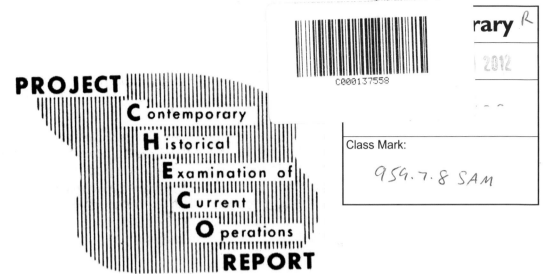

THE AIR WAR IN VIETNAM
1968 - 1969 (U)

1 APRIL 1970

HQ PACAF

Directorate, Tactical Evaluation
CHECO Division

Prepared by:
MR K. SAMS
LT COL J. SCHLIGHT
LT COL R. F. KOTT
LT COL M. J. MENDELSOHN
MAJ P. D. CAINE
Project CHECO 7th AF, DOAC

PROJECT CHECO REPORTS

The counterinsurgency and unconventional warfare environment of Southeast Asia has resulted in the employment of USAF airpower to meet a multitude of requirements. The varied applications of airpower have involved the full spectrum of USAF aerospace vehicles, support equipment, and manpower. As a result, there has been an accumulation of operational data and experiences that, as a priority, must be collected, documented, and analyzed as to current and future impact upon USAF policies, concepts, and doctrine.

Fortunately, the value of collecting and documenting our SEA experiences was recognized at an early date. In 1962, Hq USAF directed CINCPACAF to establish an activity that would be primarily responsive to Air Staff requirements and direction, and would provide timely and analytical studies of USAF combat operations in SEA.

Project CHECO, an acronym for Contemporary Historical Examination of Current Operations, was established to meet this Air Staff requirement. Managed by Hq PACAF, with elements at Hq 7AF and 7AF/13AF, Project CHECO provides a scholarly, "on-going" historical examination, documentation, and reporting on USAF policies, concepts, and doctrine in PACOM. This CHECO report is part of the overall documentation and examination which is being accomplished. Along with the other CHECO publications, this is an authentic source for an assessment of the effectiveness of USAF airpower in PACOM.

MILTON B. ADAMS, Major General, USAF
Chief of Staff

ii

REPLY TO
ATTN OF   DOTEC   1 April 1970

SUBJECT   Project CHECO Report, "The Air War in Vietnam, 1968-1969" (U)

TO   SEE DISTRIBUTION PAGE

1. Attached is a SECRET NOFORN document. It shall be transported, stored, safeguarded, and accounted for in accordance with applicable security directives. SPECIAL HANDLING REQUIRED, NOT RELEASABLE TO FOREIGN NATIONALS. The information contained in this document will not be disclosed to foreign nationals or their representatives. Retain or destroy in accordance with AFR 205-1. Do not return.

2. This letter does not contain classified information and may be declassified if attachment is removed from it.

FOR THE COMMANDER IN CHIEF

MAURICE L. GRIFFITH, Colonel, USAF   1 Atch
Chief, CHECO Division   Proj CHECO Rprt (S/NF),
Directorate, Tactical Evaluation   1 Apr 70
DCS/Operations

DISTRIBUTION LIST

1. SECRETARY OF THE AIR FORCE

    a. SAFAA 1
    b. SAFLL 1
    c. SAFOI 2

2. HEADQUARTERS USAF

    a. AFBSA 1

    b. AFCCS
       (1) AFCCSSA 1
       (2) AFCVC 1
       (3) AFCAV 1
       (4) AFCHO 1

    c. AFCSA
       (1) AFCSAG. 1
       (2) AFCSAMI 1

    d. AFGOA 2

    e. AFIGO
       (1) AFISI 3
       (2) AFISP 1

    f. AFMSG 1

    g. AFNIATC 5

    h. AFAAC 1
       (1) AFAMAI. 1

    i. AFODC
       (1) AFOAP 1
       (2) AFOCC 1
       (3) AFOCE 1
       (5) AFOMO 1

    j. AFPDC
       (1) AFPDPSS 1
       (2) AFPMDG. 1
       (3) AFPDW 1

    k. AFRDC 1
       (1) AFRDD 1
       (2) AFRDQ 1
       (3) AFRDQRC 1
       (4) AFRDR 1

    l. AFSDC
       (1) AFSLP 1
       (2) AFSME 1
       (3) AFSMS 1
       (4) AFSPD 1
       (5) AFSSS 1
       (6) AFSTP 1

    m. AFTAC 1

    n. AFXDC 1
       (1) AFXDO 1
       (2) AFXDOC. 1
       (3) AFXDOD. 1
       (4) AFXDOL. 1
       (5) AFXOP 1
       (6) AFXOSL. 1
       (7) AFXOSN. 1
       (8) AFXOSO. 1
       (9) AFXOSS. 1
     (10) AFXOSV. 1
     (11) AFXOTR. 1
     (12) AFXOTW. 1
     (13) AFXOTZ. 1
     (14) AFXOXY. 1
     (15) AFXPD 6
         (a) AFXPPGS 3

TABLE OF CONTENTS

FOOTNOTES   <u>Page</u>

FOREWORD

The character of the U.S. military effort in Vietnam and the role of airpower in support of that effort changed markedly between January 1968--when the enemy launched his greatest offensive of the war--and December 1969, when the pace of the war had slowed appreciably. The enemy had suffered a major defeat in his early 1968 offensive; U.S. bombing of North Vietnam had been halted; and peace negotiations were begun in Paris. The out-country air effort shifted to strike against enemy infiltration routes in Southern Laos and support of Royal Lao Forces in Northern Laos. The U.S. and Allied ground forces in the Republic of Vietnam (RVN) operated under a strategy emphasizing reconnaissance and undercutting the enemy infrastructure. The combination of air interdiction in Laos and ground and air attrition of the enemy logistics base and infrastructure in RVN gradually eroded the enemy's capabilities, allowing the RVN political and military establishments to expand control of the countryside and take a greater role in combat.

This CHECO Report documents the role of airpower in this critical period of the war. It describes the various elements of the USAF air capability and how they were employed in support of United States strategy in Vietnam.

CHAPTER I

OVERVIEW

At the beginning of 1968, fighting in Vietnam was at its fiercest. The forces of the North Vietnamese Army (NVA) and the Viet Cong (VC) were at their high point of effectiveness. Main Force and Local Force units with their supporting elements--porters, guides, communications, intelligence, supply caches--were primed to support large-scale operations. [1] Mass attacks on the outpost of Khe Sanh in the northwest corner of the Republic of Vietnam (RVN) began in January, and in February, the enemy, in his largest onslaught of the war, was battling in the streets of Saigon, Hue, and practically every major city in Vietnam. The enemy was beaten down, but the results of the offensive were to change the whole character of the U.S. commitment and the nature of the war itself.

Against the backdrop of a halt in the bombing of North Vietnam (NVN), negotiations in Paris began, large search and destroy operations gave way to attacks on the enemy infrastructure, and the interdiction program against enemy movement on the Ho Chi Minh Trail in Laos was stepped up. The air effort shifted from an allocation of 70 percent of the sorties in-country and 30 percent out-country to 55 percent out-country and 45 percent in-country. [2] By the end of 1969, the war was in the sixth month of its longest lull. The U.S. had begun withdrawing its forces, a program for Vietnamization of the war had started, the Republic of Vietnam was expanding its influence in the countryside, and U.S. casualties were

1

sharply reduced.

Airpower played a critical role in the events between January 1968 and December 1969, a period of significance in which strategy and goals of both sides changed considerably. In the enemy's February, May, and August offensives of 1968, the firepower available in tac air and B-52 strikes was directed against massed enemy assaults where airpower could be used most efficiently. According to Gen. George S. Brown, Commander, Seventh Air Force, "Khe Sanh and the Tet Offensive were the beginning of the end for the communists in their military operations in RVN."[3/]

The hammering down of these offensives by combined ground and air action, coupled with the success of the air interdiction program in the southern part of North Vietnam (Route Package I), rendered the majority of North Vietnamese Army units ineffective and created the security conditions in Vietnam in late 1968 which allowed Gen. Creighton W. Abrams, Jr., Commander, U.S. Military Assistance Command, Vietnam (COMUSMACV), to institute a new strategy. This called for an "accelerated pacification program" which essentially focused friendly effort on attacks against the enemy's infrastructure to destroy the VC guerrilla base on which the NVA depended so heavily.[4/] According to General Abrams, the successive weakening of the enemy offensive capability in late 1968 and all of 1969 was due to the success of the Accelerated Pacification Program, in which tactical air and B-52s played an important role in RVN and Laos.^{5}

After the complete halt of bombing in NVN on 1 November 1968, the main weight of the out-country air effort was directed against the Ho Chi Minh Trail in Laos (COMMANDO HUNT I). General Abrams credited the success of COMMANDO HUNT with preventing the enemy from meeting his objectives in the rainy season of 1969 when the war entered its longest lull. He also cited tac air and B-52s, which provided the "biggest weight of firepower," as of great importance to the in-country war in terms of creating heavy enemy casualties and minimizing friendly losses. This combination of an interdiction effort in Laos with highly potent air support of pacification goals in Vietnam was believed by General Abrams to be critical to the successful meeting of U.S. objectives-- even more than the decisive defeats handed the enemy when he emerged into the open en masse during the early 1968 offensives. There were day-by-day attacks on the logistical-communications base of the enemy, normally called his infrastructure. Such measures as air attacks, increased police activity, small unit ambushes, population control measures, and greater use of RVN Local Forces in village pacification and security replaced the strategy of employing division-sized U.S. and RVN forces in large-scale search and destroy operations. The results of this change of strategy, which began in mid-1968, were clearly evident at the end of 1969. RVN control of the countryside was greater than ever and enemy initiatives were on the decline, allowing the U.S. to begin a withdrawal by transferring more and more of the fighting to the Republic of Vietnam

Armed Forces (RVNAF).

There were several major developments which, in the view of COMUSMACV, permitted airpower to function more efficiently than ever in support of overall objectives. Of considerable importance was the institution of the MACV Single Manager for Air in March 1968. According to General Abrams, centralized management of the air effort enabled him personally to conduct operations more efficiently:[6/]

> "...From my level, power can be moved with ease in the area which includes BARREL ROLL /Northern Laos/, STEEL TIGER /the Lao panhandle/, and South Vietnam. Wherever the enemy puts the heat on, whether it's the Plain of Jars or Duc Lap, it's only a matter of hours before tremendous shifts of power can be made...with no long warning to the enemy. The centralized control of the application of power is critical to the efficient use of power...."

Another important element which led to improved use of the air capability, according to General Abrams, was the combination of an integrated all-source intelligence system for better targeting and an integrated all-resource reaction to this intelligence:[7/]

> "...Over a two-year period, all-source targeting has been steadily and dramatically improved. Our goal is "steel on the target" and that takes good targeting. In the Air Force, this is especially important in the interdiction program.
>
> "...Also, you must have an integrated, all-resource reaction to this intelligence, including tac air, B-52s, and gunships. These must be organized to strike so that all of them can be applied and integrated. If so, it will provide a terrifying and powerful blow to the enemy over a

short period of time. This aspect of our operations has improved significantly.

"The air is a really powerful weapon. To use this power effectively, you need both integrated all-source intelligence and an integrated all-resource reaction...."

The improvement cited by COMUSMACV in the all-source intelligence system meant that the tremendous firepower provided by the Air Force could be more damaging to an enemy who used camouflage, cover, and dispersion with great skill. During 1968 and 1969, the number of strike sorties was at an all-time high, reaching a peak of 37,000 throughout Southeast Asia in July 1969. Since February 1965, when the U.S. committed its jet aircraft to in-country bombing and started bombing North Vietnam, more than 1,345,000 strike sorties were flown by 7AF, U.S. Navy, U.S. Marine Corps, and SAC aircraft, dropping more than three and a half million tons of bombs. The cumulative impact of this air effort, particularly in 1968 and 1969 when targeting was improved, created a severely inhibited environment for the enemy, forcing him to make greater use of sanctuary camps outside RVN and to change his tactics. To move from the border camps toward objectives in RVN, he had to run the air gauntlet; if he massed his forces around Special Forces Camps or other friendly targets, he made a prime target for airstrikes. Within Vietnam, the VC guerrilla infrastructure--on which he depended for preparation of the battlefield by recruiting porters, pre-stocking caches, preparing bunkers, and evacuating the wounded and dead--was weakened.[8] The enemy faced a major dilemma.

To achieve significant military results, he had to mass and move through exposed areas where he was vulnerable to attacks by heavy firepower, including airstrikes. On the other hand, his inactivity allowed for persistent ground and air attacks upon his VC guerrilla support structure.

Another key element in the air support of COMUSMACV's strategy in 1969 was the USAF reconnaissance effort, both photo reconnaissance and visual reconnaissance (VR), particularly the VR role of the USAF Forward Air Controllers (FACs) in Southeast Asia. General Abrams recognized the need for photo reconnaissance in the total intelligence effort. With its black and white coverage, plus color, camouflage photos, and infra-red (IR), it provided an input which could not be obtained elsewhere. Generals Abrams and Brown had high praise for the FACs who flew many types of aircraft on visual reconnaissance, from the tiny O-1 Bird Dog to the powerful F-4 Phantom--depending upon the environment. General Abrams particularly noted the FAC's great importance in operations on the borders of Laos and Cambodia: "In these border areas, you're not in the ball game unless a FAC is there." He further stated:[9]

> "...He makes sure you're doing what is authorized and
> not guessing. He takes the guesswork out of the
> operation. The FACs have made a real contribution
> because they are seasoned professionals. FACs don't
> get lost...."

Also critical to success of the new strategy, begun in the fall of 1968, was the role of USAF airlift, ranging from the long-range airlift

0-1, OV-10, 0-2 Aircraft (Top to Bottom)
FIGURE 2

of the Military Airlift Command (MAC), which carried high value cargo, passengers, and hospitalized patients, to the short run tactical airlift by C-130s, C-123s, and C-7s. General Abrams cited movement of the 1st Air Cavlary Division from I Corps to Northern III Corps in late October 1968. The decision to transport this unit was made at 1730 hours on a Saturday, with plans calling for the move to start on the following Monday and be completed in 15 days. By Monday afternoon, the first units of the 1st Air Cav to be moved were in contact with the enemy in III Corps, and the rest of the move was completed on time. Considering that the 1st Air Cav with its 400 plus helicopters was a heavily equipped unit, this move demonstrated the efficiency of USAF combat airlift. Airlift was also essential to maintenance of the Civilian Irregular Defenses Group (CIDG) camps strung across the length of Vietnam, being capable of airlanding troops and supplies and, where this was not possible, employing airdrops. 10/

The importance attached to the USAF airlift was reflected in the strong objections raised by MACV when Seventh Air Force tried to reduce it. The number of C-130s used in SEA steadily declined by a third from mid-1968 to the end of 1969, when some 55 of these versatile aircraft were being used. Improved efficiency in control, as well as the reduced U.S. ground force commitment, made this reduction possible; further cutbacks were planned as the U.S. withdrew more ground forces. However, General Brown, as well as General Abrams, recognized that the airlift capability was "absolutely essential" to the support of U.S. forces in advanced positions and to the movement of people and supplies.[11/]

Major political decisions made in 1968 and 1969 influenced the role of airpower in support of U.S. strategy in Southeast Asia. Of prime importance were the partial bombing halt of 1 April 1968, which moved the locus of the air interdiction effort southward into the lower part of North Vietnam (Route Package I), and the total halt of 1 November, which brought the effort even farther south into the Laos panhandle.

After the initial bombing halt, a concentrated interdiction program was conducted against enemy lines of communications (LOCs) in Route Package I between July and October, which successfully stopped the enemy from moving into RVN. After the total bombing halt on 1 November 1968, COMMANDO HUNT I, a dry season interdiction program in Laos, using IGLOO WHITE sensor technology, followed up the success of the Route Package I Program. The interdiction inhibited enemy movement through Laos, limiting throughput to less than 20 percent of the input into the system. This latter success was due to effects of monsoon weather on the Laotian LOCs and to the earlier bombing of North Vietnam, because the enemy had not been able to pre-position supplies and trucks in the north for the move south when the roads dried. However, in preparation for the 1969-1970 dry season, the enemy freed from air attacks in North Vietnam for a year, was able to get a head start, moving his supplies, trucks, and fuel storage areas to the border in readiness for the move south through

8

Laos. This advantage, linked with improved antiaircraft defenses, an enlarged road system, fuel pipelines from NVN to Laos, and the necessary diversion of available strike sorties to counter heightened enemy activity in northern Laos made the friendly situation less favorable than in the previous dry season. Enemy infiltration through Cambodia into III and IV Corps in 1969 was relatively uninhibited until supplies and men crossed the border into Vietnam, and an increased NVN presence in IV Corps at the end of the year reflected this advantage held by the enemy.[12]

Despite the advantages provided to the enemy by the cessation of bombing in North Vietnam and his relative freedom to use Cambodia and Laos as a sanctuary free from ground attack, his military situation was gradually eroding from his "high point" of February 1968. Both General Abrams and General Brown recognized the importance of a combined air-ground effort to the continuing deterioration of the enemy situation. The constant pressure placed by air on enemy infiltration efforts and the forced attrition of those men and supplies which got through were essential to Allied success. While the interdiction of infiltration routes was primarily an air function, the attrition of enemy resources in RVN was a joint air-ground operation. This attrition was most successful when ground forces, operating on long-range reconnaissance missions, located enemy caches and flushed out enemy soldiers, making them more vulnerable to air-strikes. This success was clearly demonstrated in the A Shau Valley campaigns of early 1969 where U.S. and ARVN units, supported by airpower, were unearthing approximately ten tons of enemy materiel daily--materiel which had survived the interdiction effort. The air and ground efforts were very closely related. Air attacks could not substitute for ground operations in getting at the enemy infrastructure and his caches.[13/]

The reduction of the U.S. ground effort toward the end of 1969 and early 1970, such as in the A Shau Valley campaigns, was a source of concern to General Brown. Interdiction to be most successful was a two-ended task involving both air and ground operations. The enemy, forced by airstrikes to move his supplies inside RVN by porters and bicycles, had begun building stockpile caches. The reduction of U.S. ground strength in Vietnam was quite obviously something which could work to the detriment of the in-country part of this task.[14/]

The problem which this detriment would present to the U.S. policy for withdrawal from the Vietnam conflict through Vietnamization was pointed out by General Brown:[15/]

> "...We will have improved the Vietnamese armed forces but their capability will be considerably less than what we have today. Therefore, our task is to trim the security problem to a scale that the Vietnamese can handle. In the time we have left, however long that is, we must make pacification work....We're making some progress. Communist recruiting is falling off. As their main forces are being pushed back into the jungle and across the borders, the police and ARVN come in to take a firmer hold."

Thus, at the end of 1969, it was clear that the course of events in the future would be greatly influenced by political considerations. The enemy had been thwarted by military force from his goals. In the process of withdrawing its armed forces and building up those of the Vietnamese, the U.S. hoped that it could do so without upsetting the still fragile, yet steadily growing control of the country by the Government of Vietnam (GVN).

CHAPTER II

POSTURE AND GOALS

The military strategy of the United States in Vietnam was to seek out and destroy Communist forces and infrastructure by expanded, offensive military operations and to assist the Government of Vietnam in building an independent, viable nation. The strategy outside the Republic of Vietnam in this period was to take the war to the enemy in Laos and North Vietnam by selective application of U.S. air and naval power to reduce the capability of Hanoi to support military operations in South Vietnam. Major military and political developments in 1968 and 1969 resulted in several changes in goals supporting this strategy.[1] In South Vietnam, the goal of enhancing effectiveness of the Republic of Vietnam Armed Forces was elevated to highest priority on the Commander-in-Chief, Pacific Command (CINCPAC) listing of goals. The bombing halts of 1968 in North Vietnam changed the goals for the out-country effort, limiting the out-country air war to Laos. The specific goals for the air war in 1969 paralleled those of CINCPAC. These were to:[2]

- Organize, equip, modernize, and employ the VNAF to achieve a maximum state of combat effectiveness.

- Inflict more losses on the enemy than he can replace.

- Assist in increasing the percentage of the population and territory under GVN control through an expanded pacification effort.

- Reduce the ability of the enemy to conduct ground

attacks or attacks by fire against population
centers, economic areas, and bases.

. Deny the maximum number of base area sanctuaries
in RVN to the enemy by their destruction or continual neutralization.

. Assist in restoring and serving to the greatest
extent possible the road, railroad, and waterway
LOCs.

. Assist in neutralizing the enemy infrastructure
in all pacification priority areas.

. Coordinate intelligence collection and counter-
intelligence activities to the maximum extent
possible.

Seventh Air Force tasks to accomplish these objectives encompassed
air defense, close air support, tactical airlift, interdiction, maintenance of air supremacy, reconnaissance, targeting, intelligence, air-
sea rescue, civic action, psychological operations, VNAF assistance and
enhancement, and herbicide operations.[3]

The fundamental enemy objective in RVN was the "creation of a
politico-military climate conducive to the establishment of a Communist
government."[4] Military force was the primary means of achieving that
goal. VC and NVA tactics consisted mainly of general harassment, terror-
ism, sabotage, psychological warfare, interdiction, and small-scale
attacks on isolated camps and villages. But the 1968 Tet offensive was
a massive departure from these tactics as the enemy made a major bid for
a quick victory by striking with massed forces throughout the Republic of
Vietnam. Enemy planning called for the continued maintenance of a

13

credible large-scale threat in order to provide the greatest possible latitude in the conduct of offensive operations. [5]

A major innovation in the control of air operations occurred in March 1968 when the battle for Khe Sanh dramatically revealed the lack of single management for the application of airpower. [6] Acting on COMUSMACV's proposal, CINCPAC approved the Single Management System (SMS), and it was established on 8 March 1968. [7] Under the system, the Deputy COMUSMACV Operations for Air (Comdr, 7AF) integrated the planning, coordination, and control of all in-country air resources, including those of the U.S. Marine Corps (USMC) and U.S. Navy (USN). For the first time, the air war could be viewed, pursued, and coherently coordinated from a single vantage point. The unifying element was the Tactical Air Control System (TACS), where the "operational direction" prerogative gave 7AF authority to issue frag orders, order scrambles, divert aircraft, and direct engagement of air or ground targets (Fig. 3). [8]

While in-country air operations were managed through the 7AF Tactical Air Control Center (TACC), all out-country air operations were managed through BLUE CHIP, the Seventh Air Force Control Center (7AFCC). BLUE CHIP controlled air operations over NVN, air support of Royal Lao Government (RLG) forces in northern Laos, and the air interdiction campaign against the NVN LOCs through southern Laos into RVN. Seventh Air Force had operational control of U.S. strike forces in Thailand as well as in RVN. Before flying into Laos, USN and USMC strikes were coordinated with

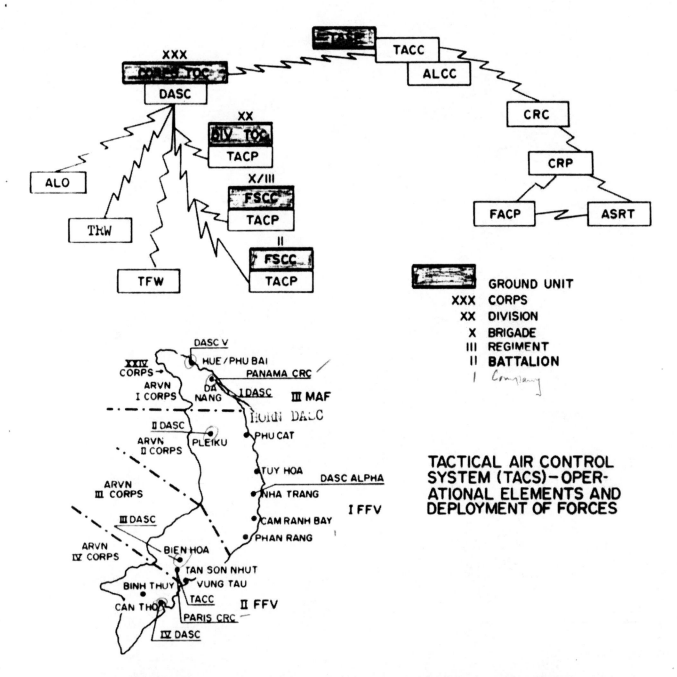

THE UPPER ILLUSTRATION DEPICTS THE OPERATIONAL ELEMENTS OF THE TACS WHILE THE LOWER FIGURE SHOWS THEIR LOCATION IN SVN. THE TACS PERMITS COMMAND TO SHIFT, REDEPLOY AND CONCENTRATE ITS FORCE TO FIT MOST PRESSING REQUIREMENTS. COORDINATION BETWEEN AIR AND GROUND FORCES IS BUILT INTO THE TACS PROVIDING MAXIMUM FLEXIBILITY FOR AIR SUPPORT.

FIGURE 3

Tactical Air Control Center at Hq 7AF

FIGURE 4

7AF. In effect, the operational control arrangements for the out-country air approximated the Single Management System used in South Vietnam.[9/]

The magnitude of the management of airpower expanded with the steadily growing commitment. In 1964, the USAF had 230 aircraft in SEA. By 1967, that figure had increased to approximately 1,350. Army aviation greatly expanded during the period reaching more than 2,000 aircraft, mostly Bell UH-1 helicopters.[10/] By 1968, USAF strength leveled and remained fairly stable until the end of 1969. Army aviation, on the other hand, continued to grow with the UH-1 (Iroquois), popularly known as Huey, continuing to dominate its inventory by almost 53 percent.[11/] At the end of 1968, one-half of the Marine Corps' total aviation force was deployed in Vietnam, amounting to 27 of its 56 aircraft squadrons and 6 of its 14 Hawk missile batteries.[12/] By the end of 1969, the Marine commitment was reduced to 24 squadrons with further reductions scheduled for CY 70.[13/]

In December 1969, there were 6,960 combat and support aircraft based in South Vietnam, Thailand, and aboard carriers in the Western Pacific.[14/] These statistics show combined aircraft force levels at the beginning, middle, and end of the period of this report.[15/]

TOTAL COMBAT AND SUPPORT AIRCRAFT IN SEA

	JAN 1968	JAN 1969	DEC 1969
USAF	1,702	1,759	1,765
USMC	585	536	367
USN	399	307	311
USA	3,004	3,645	4,089
VNAF	366	361	420
RAAF	8	8	8
TOTAL	6,064	6,616	6,960

Soon after the 1 November 1968 bombing halt in NVN, the U.S. Navy's Western Pacific force of five carriers was reduced to four, two assigned to YANKEE STATION (approximately 18° N, 107° 40' E) in the Gulf of Tonkin, one in the Sea of Japan, and another in port. The number of aircraft at YANKEE STATION varied from 140 to 180, depending upon size and type of the carriers; the total aircraft at the four Western Pacific carriers averaged 334 in December 1969.[16/]

In the Republic of Vietnam in 1969, under 7AF, there were six Tactical Fighter Wings, one Tactical Reconnaissance Wing, two Special Operations (formerly Air Commando) Wings, and one airlift division consisting of one tactical wing and one Special Operations Wing (Fig. 5). In Thailand, under the Deputy Commander, 7AF/13AF, there were three Tactical Fighter Wings, two Reconnaissance Wings, two Combat Support Groups, and one

ORGANIZATION, 7th AIR FORCE AND 7/13th AIR FORCE

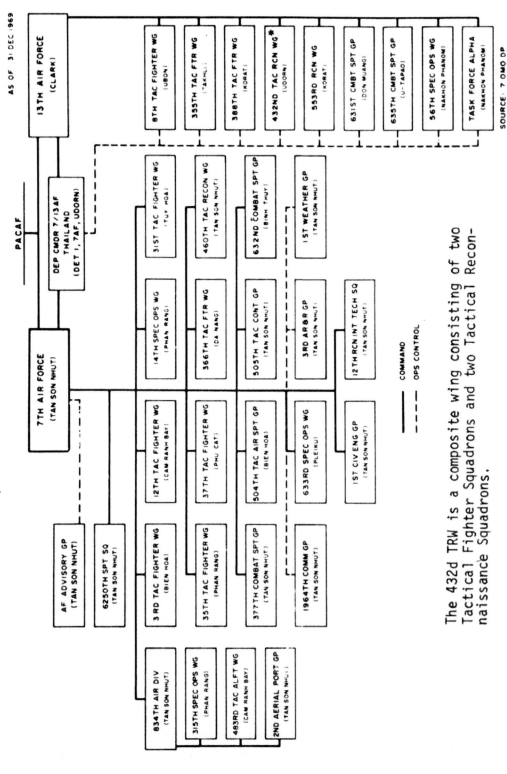

AS OF 31 DEC 1969

SOURCE: 7 OMO DP

COMMAND

OPS CONTROL

The 432d TRW is a composite wing consisting of two Tactical Fighter Squadrons and two Tactical Reconnaissance Squadrons.

FIGURE 5

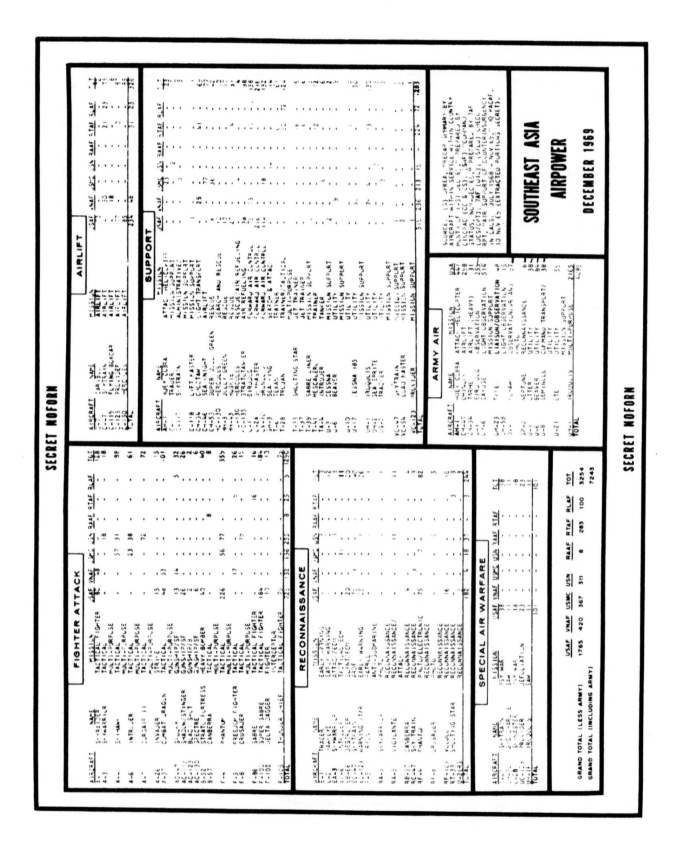

FIGURE 6

F-111 Aircraft
FIGURE 7

Special Operations Wing throughout 1968 and 1969. Task Force Alpha (TFA), a wing level agency which operated the Infiltration Surveillance Center based on sensor technology at Nakhon Phanom, Thailand, became operational on 1 December 1967.[17/]

Figure 6 shows the total SEA air assets divided among the five major functional roles.[18/] Army air is shown separately. The air assets shown in the figure varied only slightly during 1968 and 1969. The most notable changes were the addition of SAC B-52s at U-Tapao in January 1968,[19/] the introduction of OV-10s at Da Nang, Bien Hoa, and Pleiku in July 1968,[20/] and the introduction of AC-119, AC-130, and AC-123 gunships.

From 17 March to 19 November 1968, a combat evaluation of the F-111 (called COMBAT LANCER) was conducted at Takhli RTAFB, Thailand. The unit, consisting of six F-111s, flew 55 combat missions over NVN to evaluate the low level, night/adverse-weather penetration and attack capability.[21/] Three aircraft were lost during the evaluation.[22/]

The geographic distribution of the USAF forces is also shown in Figure 6. The air order of battle (AOB) of the combat aircraft shown is that of 31 December 1969 and is typical of the two years covered by this report.

During the same period, the number of personnel assigned to 7AF units varied from a low of 44,812 to a peak of 49,823, averaging approximately 48,000.[23/] Total Air Force military personnel in RVN, including TDY personnel, rose gradually at a fairly constant rate from 56,468 in January 1968 to 63,349 in September 1969, when it dropped abruptly to 57,468 by

17

December.[24/] Total USAF personnel strength, including U.S. civilians and local nationals, was apportioned among ten major bases and other outlying locations in RVN (Fig. 8); the strength stayed constant (it varied almost imperceptibly) during the period of this report at around 68,500 until October 1969, when the figure began to decline noticeably.[25/] In Thailand, USAF military personnel increased in 1968 from 28,250 to about 36,000 and leveled there in 1969. The USAF accounted for 76 percent of all Department of Defense (DOD) military personnel assigned in Thailand in 1968 and 1969. In South Vietnam, USAF personnel accounted for only 11 percent of the total U.S. military force.[26/]

The enemy's AOB consisted of 262 jet aircraft in December 1969, more than half of which were based in China.[27/] In 1968, when NVN bases were subjected to U.S. attack, all but a small alert force had been positioned out-country in China. After the bombing halts of 1 April and 1 November 1968, the North Vietnamese rehabilitated damaged airfields and improved facilities. A substantial number of the NVN force redeployed from China before the end of 1968. The MIG order of battle increased slightly during 1968 and was made formidable by acquisition of additional MIG 21 (Fishbed F) interceptors, constituting more than one-fourth of the North Vietnamese Air Force (NVAF) fighter force in late 1969.[28/]

USAF Thailand-based aircraft operated mainly in Laos, both in BARREL ROLL (BR) and STEEL TIGER (SL) (Fig. 9). The SAC B-52s were targeted into Laos and RVN. Carrier-based USN aircraft in the Gulf of Tonkin

USAF AIRCRAFT UNITS IN RVN -- THAILAND
COMBAT ORIENTED

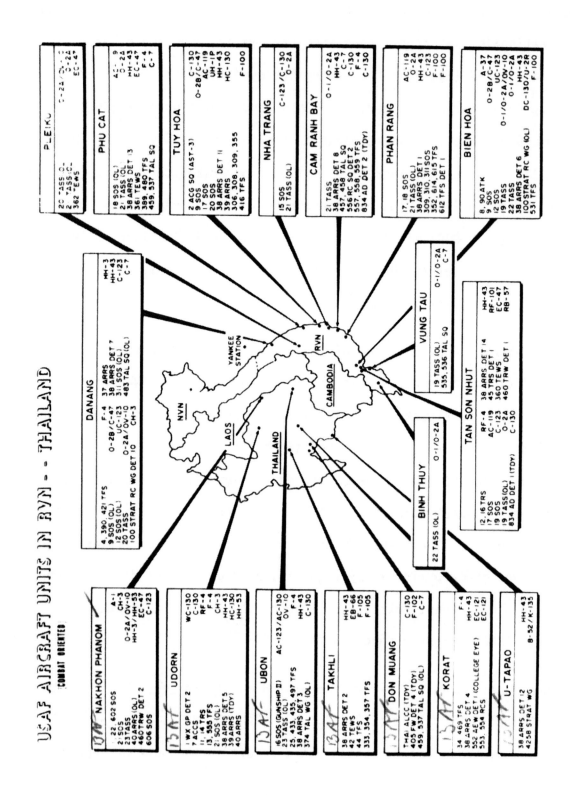

PLEIKU
20 TASS O-	O-2A/O-1
2 TASS, O-	O-2A
362 TEWS	EC-47

PHU CAT
18 SOS (OL)	AC-119
21 TASS (OL)	O-2A
38 ARRS DET 13	HH-43
361 TEWS	EC-47
389, 480 TFS	F-4
459, 537 TAL SQ	C-7

TUY HOA
2 ACG SQ (AST-31)	C-130
9 SOS	O-2B/C-47
17 SOS	AC-119
20 SOS	UH-1P
39 ARRS	HH-43
38 ARRS DET 11	HC-130
306, 308, 309, 355	
416 TFS	F-100

NHA TRANG
15 SOS	C-123/C-130
21 TASS (OL)	O-2A

CAM RANH BAY
21 TASS	O-1/O-2A
38 ARRS DET 8	HH-43
457, 458 TAL SQ	C-7
556 RC SQ DET 2	C-130
557, 558, 559 TFS	F-4
834 AD DET 2 (TDY)	C-130

PHAN RANG
17, 18 SOS	AC-119
21 TASS (OL)	O-2A
38 ARRS DET 1	HH-43
309, 310, 311 SOS	C-123
352, 614, 615 TFS	F-100
612 TFS DET 1	F-100

BIEN HOA
8, 90 ATK	A-37
9 SOS	O-2B/C-47
12 SOS	UC-123
19 TASS	O-1/O-2A/OV-10
22 TASS	O-1/O-2A
38 ARRS DET 6	HH-43
100 STRAT RC WG (OL)	DC-130/U-2R
531 TFS	F-100

DANANG
4, 390, 421 TFS	F-4
9 SOS (OL)	O-2B/C-47
12 SOS (OL)	UC-123
20 TASS	O-2A/OV-10
100 STRAT RC WG DET 10	CH-3
37 ARRS	HH-3
38 ARRS DET 7	HH-43
311 SOS (OL)	C-123
483 TAL SQ (OL)	C-7

YANKEE STATION

NVN

LAOS

THAILAND

RVN

CAMBODIA

VUNG TAU
19 TASS (OL)	O-1/O-2A
535, 536 TAL SQ	C-7

TAN SON NHUT
12, 16 TRS	RF-4
17 SOS	AC-119
19 SOS	C-123
19 TASS (OL)	O-2A
834 AD DET 1 (TDY)	C-130
38 ARRS DET 14	HH-43
45 TRS DET 1	RF-101
360 TEWS	EC-47
460 TRW DET 1	RB-57

BINH THUY
22 TASS (OL)	O-1/O-2A

NAKHON PHANOM
1, 22, 602 SOS	A-1
2 SOS	CH-3
23 TASS	O-2A/OV-10
40 ARRS (OL)	HH-3/HH-53
460 TRW DET 2	EC-47
606 SOS	C-123

UDORN
1 WX GP DET 2	WC-130
7 ACCS	C-130
11, 14 TRS	RF-4
13, 555 TFS	F-4
21 SOS (OL)	CH-3
38 ARRS DET 5	HH-43
39 ARRS	HC-130
40 ARRS	HH-53

UBON
16 SOS (GUNSHIP II)	AC-123/AC-130
23 TASS (OL)	OV-10
25, 433, 435, 497 TFS	F-4
38 ARRS DET 3	HH-43
374 TAL WG (OL)	C-130

TAKHLI
38 ARRS DET 2	HH-43
42 TEWS	EB-66
44 TFS	F-105
333, 354, 357 TFS	F-105

DON MUANG
THAI ALCC (TDY)	C-130
405 FW DET 4 (TDY)	F-102
459, 537 TAL SQ (OL)	C-7

KORAT
34, 469 TFS	F-4
38 ARRS DET 4	HH-43
552 AEW DET 1 (COLLEGE EYE)	EC-121
553, 554 RCS	EC-121

U-TAPAO
38 ARRS DET 2	HH-43
4258 STRAT WG	B-52/KC-135

FIGURE 8

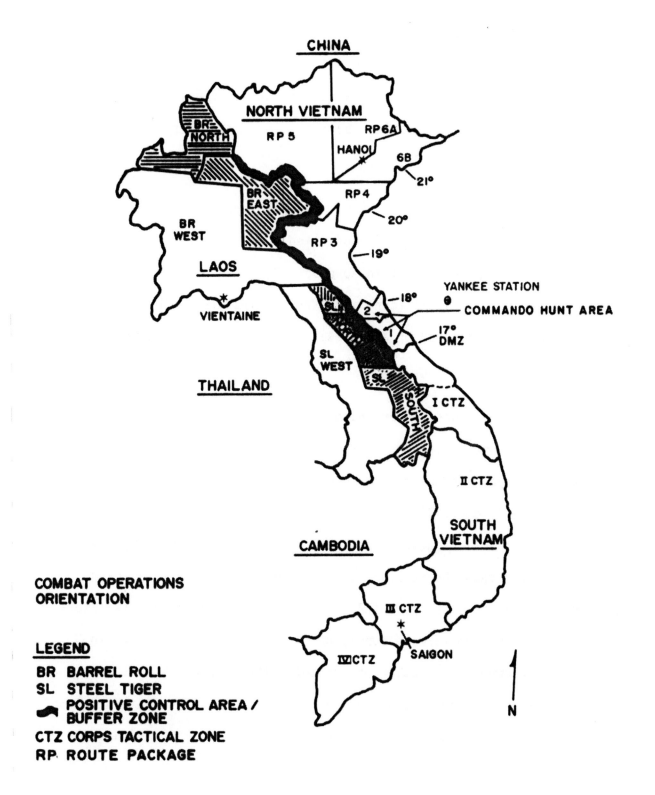

CHINA

NORTH VIETNAM

RP 5

RP 6A

HANOI

6B

21°

RP 4

20°

BR NORTH

BR EAST

BR WEST

RP 3

19°

LAOS

YANKEE STATION

18°

COMMANDO HUNT AREA

SL NORTH

VIENTAINE

2

1

17°
DMZ

SL WEST

SL SOUTH

I CTZ

THAILAND

II CTZ

SOUTH VIETNAM

CAMBODIA

III CTZ

SAIGON

COMBAT OPERATIONS
ORIENTATION

IV CTZ

LEGEND

BR BARREL ROLL
SL STEEL TIGER

POSITIVE CONTROL AREA /
BUFFER ZONE

CTZ CORPS TACTICAL ZONE

RP. ROUTE PACKAGE

N

FIGURE 9

(YANKEE STATION) flew attacks into NVN, the SL area of Laos, and in I
Corps of RVN.[29/]   The USMC, with its I Marine Air Wing (MAW) bedded down

in I Corps bases, worked primarily in I Corps and in SL in Laos. In

RVN, operations with VNAF aircraft were conducted exclusively in-country.

USAF aircraft in RVN flew missions both in- and out-country but principal-

ly in RVN.

In North Vietnam, which was the immediate supply source for enemy

activities in RVN, air operations consisted primarily of interdiction

bombing until the bombing halt in November 1968. Fighter/Attack aircraft

were targeted against significant military and industrial locations.[30/]

Enemy resistance consisted of air-to-air and ground-to-air defensive

actions.

The war in Laos was concentrated in two separate regions. The

conflict in the Northeast (BARREL ROLL) between Pathet Lao/North Vietnam

(PL/NVN) and Royal Lao Government (RLG) forces was essentially a confront-

ation of friendly guerrilla and enemy regular/unconventional forces. The

conflict was unusual because it was the guerrillas who were supported by

airpower rather than the regular forces. Here the airpower was used

primarily in close air support (CAS) roles; to a lesser extent it inter-

dicted enemy LOCs and forward supply dumps in BR. Strategically, in

terms of the combat application of airpower, the BR and RVN wars were

only indirectly related because the war in BR was a self-contained action.

The supply lines into BR from NVN were not part of the LOC net through southern Laos that fed the VC/NVA action in RVN.

The conflict on the eastern segment of the Lao panhandle (STEEL TIGER), on the other hand, was directly related to the war in South Vietnam, because the area was laced with the complex of passes, roads, and trails of the "Ho Chi Minh Trail" (Fig. 10). This region was the focus of a significant air interdiction campaign throughout 1968 and 1969. Highly sophisticated ground and airborne sensor devices enhanced intensive anti-infiltration efforts and claimed a high percentage of the USAF sortie allocation in SEA.[31/]

The air war in RVN was fought throughout the country in four corps tactical zones (CTZs). The nature of the war varied from corps to corps. I Corps was the northernmost corps area bordering NVN (DMZ) and Laos. It contained the A Shau Valley which was a favored enemy LOC and assembly area. Khe Sanh was located in I Corps, as was Hue, the ancient capital of Vietnam and the scene of heavy fighting during Tet 1968.[32/] II Corps was the largest of the four CTZs and the least densely populated; it shared a common border with Cambodia and southern Laos. Six of the ten major air bases in RVN were located there, five of them on the coastal plain near the sea. Cam Ranh Bay was one of the finest natural harbors in Southeast Asia, and the location of the largest U.S. air base.[33/] III Corps was the political center of the Republic of Vietnam. The capital, Saigon, and its servicing airport, Tan Son Nhut, were the nerve center of military and air operations in RVN. Long Binh/Bien Hoa was

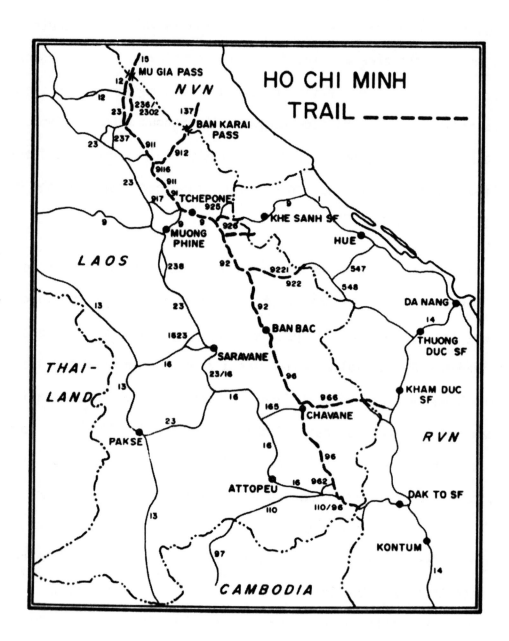

FIGURE 10

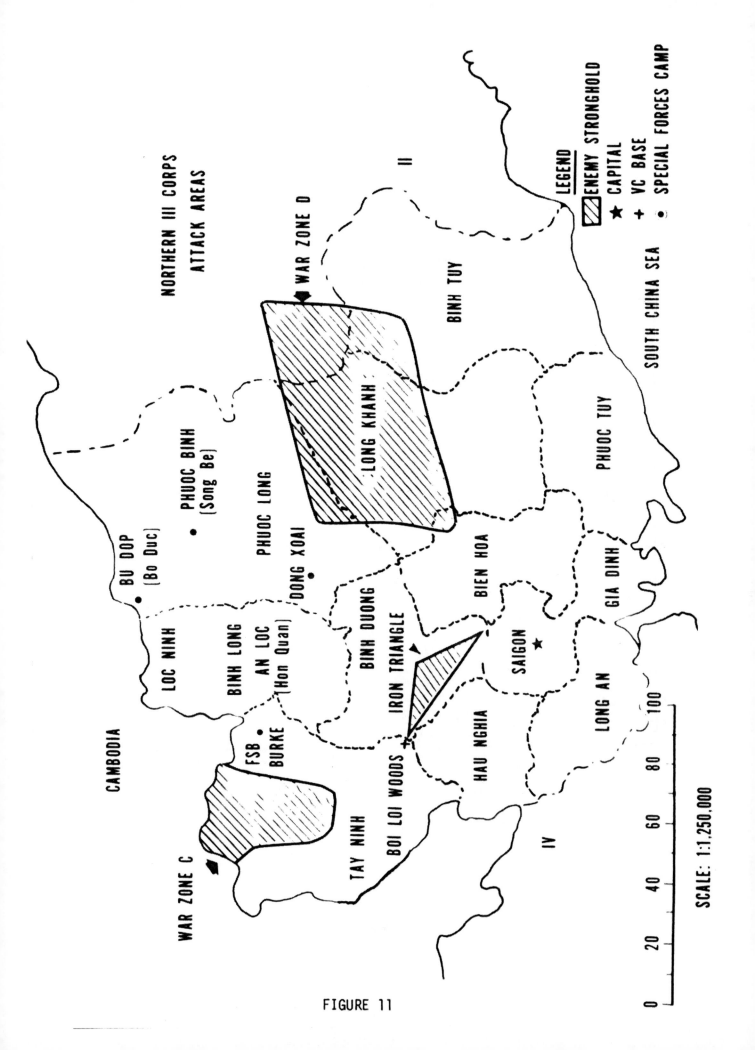

NORTHERN III CORPS
ATTACK AREAS

WAR ZONE D

II

BINH TUY

SOUTH CHINA SEA

CAMBODIA

PHUOC BINH
(Song Be)

PHUOC LONG

LONG KHANH

PHUOC TUY

BU DOP
(Bo Duc)

DONG XOAI

BIEN HOA

GIA DINH

LOC NINH

BINH LONG

AN LOC
(Hon Quan)

BINH DUONG

IRON TRIANGLE

SAIGON

FSB
BURKE

HAU NGHIA

LONG AN

TAY NINH

BOI LOI WOODS

IV

WAR ZONE C

LEGEND
ENEMY STRONGHOLD
★ CAPITAL
+ VC BASE
• SPECIAL FORCES CAMP

SCALE: 1:1,250,000

0   20   40   60   80   100

FIGURE 11

ATTACK SORTIES
(USAF & OTHERS)
1968-1969

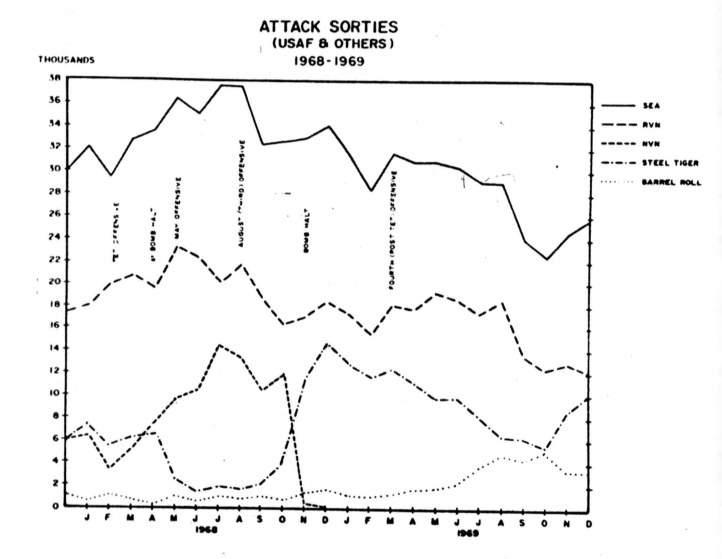

FIGURE 12

the largest free world military complex in the Republic. III Corps

also contained War Zones C and D and the Iron Triangle, well-known

enemy assembly and staging areas (Fig. 11). The Cambodian Border was

at one point only 44 km from Saigon. IV Corps was the most populous of

the four CTZs. Consisting mainly of rich alluvial flatland in the

Mekong Delta, the region was known as the "rice bowl" of South Vietnam.

Except for isolated peaks, the land does not rise over 10 feet above sea

level.[34/] The dense U-Minh forest in the Corps southwest was a well known

VC/NVA center. Riverine operations were very significant in this region.

Vietnamization of the war first began in this Corps and was more advanced

there at the end of 1969 than in other CTZs.[35/]

The geographical employment of air resources in SEA during the

period of this report is graphically illustrated in Figure 12.[36/] One of

the most striking shifts took place in November 1968 when air attacks

over the north were halted and the first COMMANDO HUNT interdiction

campaign began in the SL area of Laos. The attack sorties formerly targeted

against NVN shifted to the COMMANDO HUNT operation, leaving the overall

out-country and in-country sortie rates about the same.

The monsoon climate and its associated weather had a bearing on air

operations in SEA. The interior of SEA was dry from January through

March 1968. Rainfall then increased in the interior, reaching a maximum

in August and September. Along the northeast coast, however, the wettest

month was October. Rainfall then decreased to a minimum in December when

21

it was dry everywhere in SEA. January and February 1969 remained dry. Rainfall built up to a maximum in July in the interior. Along the northeast coast, the maximum rainfall again occurred in October when Hue received a record rainfall. December, as in 1968, was a dry month.[37/]

The requirements for in-country close air support sorties and out-country interdiction varied with the seasons and with the level of enemy activity. Figure 13 shows the monthly percent of attack sorties for both in- and out-country. Approximately 57 percent of all attacks in SEA were flown in-country. During the dry seasons, enemy activity in the STEEL TIGER interdiction area was increased.[38/]

Of the four corps in RVN, I Corps was provided the greatest number of attack sorties, while III Corps was the second most active (Fig. 14). The II, III, and IV Corps were remarkably stable during the two-year period, showing relatively little fluctuation on a monthly or annual basis. Neither the chronology of significant events listed on the chart nor the seasons appeared to have a marked effect on sortie experience. I Corps, on the other hand, seemed very sensitive to the perturbations.[39/]

Combat operations in NVN, Laos, and RVN were conducted day and night. On the average, day attack sorties accounted for 77 percent of the diurnal effort, a percentage that fluctuated no more than two percent from 1 July 1968 to 31 December 1969, when calculated on a quarterly basis.[40/]

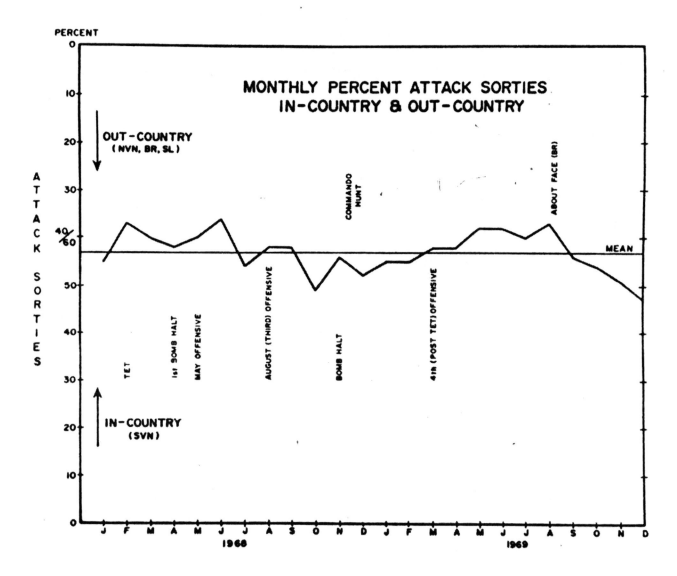

FIGURE 13

ATTACK SORTIES – REPUBLIC OF VIETNAM
1968 – 1969
I, II, III & IV CORPS

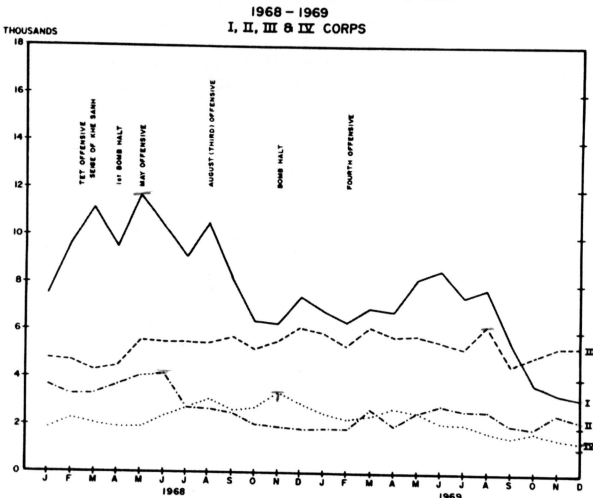

FIGURE 14

ATTACK SORTIES - REPUBLIC OF VIETNAM
USAF & OTHER - 1969

	CY 68 Avg	J	F	M	A	M	J	J	A	S	O	N	D
USAF	11302	9471	8555	9726	9351	9460	9227	8318	8614	6468	5633	6158	5669
USMC/USN	5861	5307	4882	5809	6517	6419	6222	5818	5883	3853	2825	2647	2599
RAAF	237	221	217	249	241	239	234	240	241	180	242	241	240
VNAF	2223	2069	2026	2429	2349	2912	2773	3092	3593	3022	3491	3523	3576
TOTAL	19623	17068	15680	18213	18458	19030	18456	17468	18331	13513	12191	12564	12084
VNAF % OF EFFORT	11.3	12.1	12.9	13.3	12.7	15.3	15.0	17.7	19.6	22.3	28.6	28.0	29.6

SOURCE: Interview, Capt G. H. Kent, 7AF (CPTM) with Lt Col R. F. Kott, CHECO Writer, 6 Feb 70.

FIGURE 15

VNAF furnished combat and support aircraft for missions throughout the four CTZs. In December 1969, the VNAF unit equipment (UE) inventory consisted of 446 aircraft. Of these, 114 were fighter aircraft and 16 were fixed-wing gunships, for a total of 130 attack aircraft. The remainder of the aircraft were liaison, helicopter, transport, and recon- naissance aircraft.[41/] The VNAF was steadily being improved and expanded during 1968-1969. The A-37s and the AC-47s came into the inventory, increasing VNAF combat operations, as shown by the increasing number of VNAF attack sorties:[42/]

PERCENT OF ATTACK SORTIES FLOWN BY VNAF
(1968-1969)

CORPS	1968	1969
I	4.9	4.3 -
II	3.9	16.2 +
III	24.8	34.1 +
IV	15.2	19.4 +
Avg	12.2	18.5

While the increase of 6.3 percent in 1969 seemed modest, the rate of buildup examined on a monthly basis was impressive (Fig. 15). The scaling down of the in-country war was apparent as the total attack sorties fell from 17,068 in January 1969 to 12,084 in December. VNAF participation, on the other hand, increased steadily both in absolute and percentage terms, from 2,069 to 3,576 sorties, accounting for 12.1 to 29.6 percent, respectively.

23

A prime example of Vietnamization of air operations was evident in IV Corps within the 74th VNAF Wing at Binh Thuy. During 1968 and early 1969, pilots of the 74th flew the H-34, the A-1E Skyraider, and conducted limited FAC operations in the O-1. From April to June 1969, the 74th Wing underwent a triple squadron conversion: (1) new UH-1H (Iroquois) combat assault helicopters replaced the aging H-34s, giving an increased airmobile capability to the 211th and 217th VNAF squadrons; (2) A-37B jet fighters replaced the Skyraiders in the VNAF 520th Squadron, enabling air tactical strikes to be carried out more quickly and efficiently; and (3) the 116th Squadron began handling the majority of day FAC missions in the Delta. The increased FAC capability of the VNAF resulted in a reduction of USAF air forces in IV Corps. In December 1969, the 22d Tactical Air Support Squadron (TASS) was transferred from Binh Thuy to Bien Hoa, at which time, ten of its O-1 aircraft were turned over to the VNAF. These O-1s became the nucleus of the 122d VNAF Squadron which activated in January 1970. This was the first step in Phase II of the Improvement and Modernization (I&M) program for VNAF which allowed planning for the 74th Wing's eventual air division status.[43/]

By the close of 1969, effects of the RVNAF I&M program were becoming visible in air operations. The 7AF viewed Vietnamization "equal in priority and importance to [its] combat mission,"[44/] and Gen. G. S. Brown, Commander 7AF, had no doubt that the VNAF would meet their training, activation, and equipping schedules.[45/]

24

CHAPTER III

AIR WAR IN VIETNAM

Tet Offensive and Khe Sanh

The enemy opened 1968 with an all-out attack on key US/GVN installations and population centers, hoping to achieve a complete political and military victory.[1/]   In December 1967, air reconnaissance discovered NVN troops moving into the valley around Khe Sanh, a critical juncture in I CTZ which guarded the northwestern approaches into RVN from Laos and the DMZ. In response, the Marine garrison at Khe Sanh was strengthened to 3,000 men. Enemy probes began on 21 January 1968 when a NVN battalion unsuccessfully attacked Huong Hoa, one mile from the outpost. Two days later, the enemy began a daily shelling of the base. When intelligence reports estimated the enemy strength as high as 35,000, the Marine strength was doubled to 6,000.

The MACV air plan for defending Khe Sanh was a Search-Locate-Annihilate-Monitor (SLAM) operation--NIAGARA II. For this effort, all air assets (except Marine sorties providing close air support to Marine ground forces) were placed under the control of the 7AF Commander,[2/] who exercised this control through an Airborne Battlefield Command and Control Center (ABCCC). A special Intelligence Control Center was established at 7AF to coordinate all intelligence resources for the NIAGARA operation.

On 24 January, the forward outpost (Elephant), located 18 miles SSW of Khe Sanh just inside Laos, fell to the NVN, and refugees from the camp flooded eastward along Route 9 to Lang Vei, four miles south of Khe

Sanh (Figure 17). The ABCCC and Covey FACs covered the withdrawal by

calling in airstrikes on bridges behind the fleeing Lao troops. From

this point on, friendly forces at Khe Sanh were effectively pinned down

and had to rely almost exclusively on air for defense, resupply, and

evacuation of personnel. During the first week of the siege (22-29 Jan-

uary), more than 3,000 tactical airstrikes were directed and over 200 ARC

LIGHT sorties were flown in the NIAGARA zone. The Rules of Engagement

were relaxed to permit B-52s to drop ordnance within one kilometer of

Khe Sanh.[3/]

As the second week of the siege began (30 January), the NVN launched

the country-wide Tet offensive (Fig. 18). Nearly all major cities in

RVN and 34 of the 45 provincial capitals were attacked by enemy soldiers

who had slipped into the urban centers undetected. The enemy's stated

purpose was to inspire a general uprising of the populace and to cause

the fall of the government and the creation of a new one. Before the

offensive opened, the enemy had concentrated his attacks on border areas,

thereby drawing U.S. and Army of Republic of Vietnam (ARVN) battalions

out of populated areas. The siege of Khe Sanh was one such diversion.

On the night of 29-30 January 1968, the enemy simultaneously attacked

headquarters and airfields throughout I and II Corps. Nha Trang, Kontum,

Ban Me Thuot, Qui Nhon, and Da Nang were hit. On the following night,

the attacks spread to the rest of South Vietnam. At Hue, the old imperial

VC/NVA INITIATED LARGE SCALE SIGNIFICANT ATTACKS

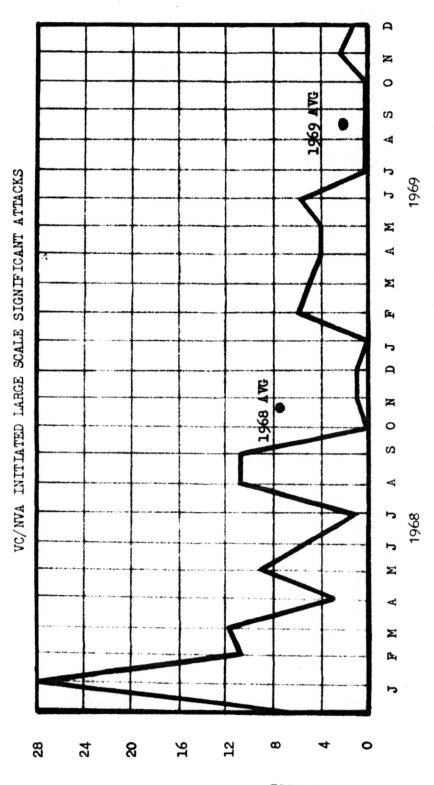

FIGURE 16

Source: "Measurement of Progress in Southeast Asia" - (1968 and 1969 Quarterlies), CINCPAC.

*Enemy Initiated Large Scale Significant Attack: Meets the criterion of size plus one or more of the other criterion, (2) through (5). (1) Size: when the enemy force is estimated to be a battalion or larger, or (2) Casualties: When the attack results in a total enemy and friendly KIA and MIA of 30 or more, or (3) Objective: When the enemy has attacked a major installation such as a base camp, airfield, a logistical installation or political/military command and control installation, or (4) Damage: When there is a loss of a substantial amount of equipment. destruction or damage to aircraft or weapons systems, or a large quantity of enemy materiel, supplies, or equipment has been captured, or (5) New Weapons, Tactics or Techniques: When the enemy introduces a new weapon or employs a new tactic or technique.

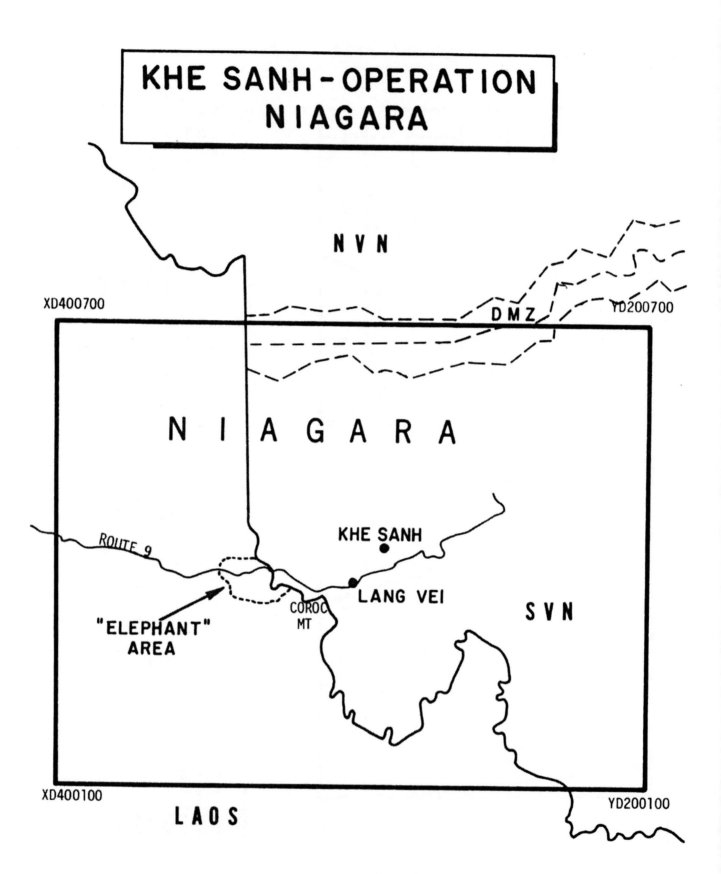

KHE SANH - OPERATION NIAGARA

NVN

XD400700

DMZ

YD200700

N I A G A R A

ROUTE 9

KHE SANH

"ELEPHANT"
AREA

COROC
MT

LANG VEI

SVN

XD400100

YD200100

LAOS

FIGURE 17

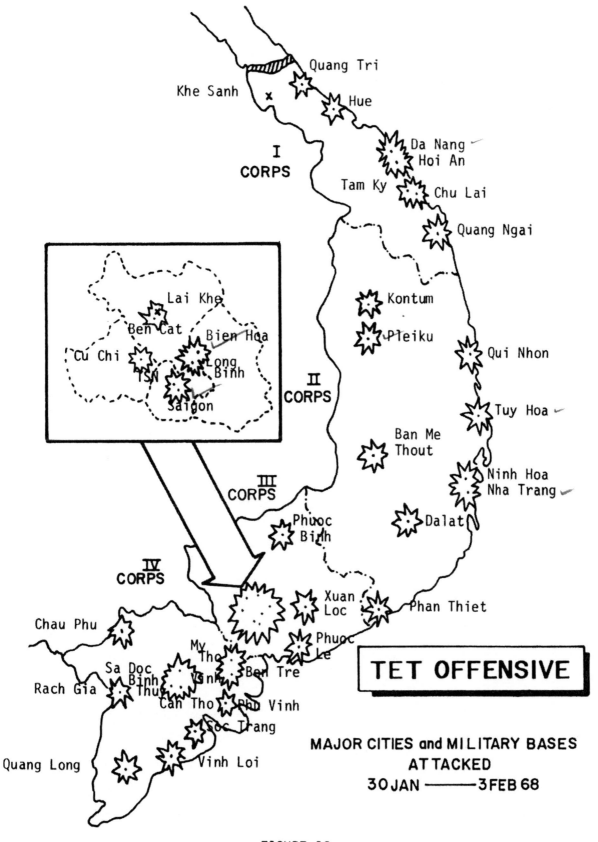

Quang Tri

Khe Sanh   ×

Hue

I
CORPS   Da Nang
                         Hoi An

                  Tam Ky   Chu Lai

                         Quang Ngai

                  Kontum

          Lai Khe   Pleiku

   Ben Cat   Bien Hoa   Qui Nhon
Cu Chi   Long
        TSN   Binh   Tuy Hoa
        Saigon   Ban Me
                    II Thout
                  CORPS   Ninh Hoa
                               Nha Trang

              III
             CORPS   Dalat
                  Phuoc
                  Binh

   IV   Xuan
  CORPS   Loc   Phan Thiet

Chau Phu   Phuoc
                  My   Le
               Tho   **TET OFFENSIVE**
   Sa Doc   Vinh Ben Tre
Rach Gia Binh   Long
        Thu   Can Tho Phu Vinh
              Soc Trang
Quang Long   **MAJOR CITIES and MILITARY BASES**
             Vinh Loi   **ATTACKED**
                         30 JAN ——— 3 FEB 68

FIGURE 18

capital, eight USAF aircraft were destroyed as 1,000 Communist soldiers seized the Citadel, the heart of the city. Whereas in I, II, and IV Corps, the enemy struck both provincial capitals and cities, in III Corps, they hit only the cities, principally Saigon and Bien Hoa. In response to the attacks, Allied units were withdrawn from the countryside to protect the cities. For the first time in the war, airstrikes were put in the cities.

The air commander had to divide his resources between Khe Sanh and other trouble spots throughout the country. Naval and Marine air forces continued to concentrate on the Khe Sanh area. Thai-based USAF aircraft were used primarily to relieve enemy pressure by interdicting the enemy's lines of communications in Laos and secondarily by directly supporting nearby Khe Sanh. RVN-based USAF aircraft were employed primarily against the enemy in urban areas and secondarily at Khe Sanh. During the first three days of the Tet offensive, the number of aircraft sorties supporting Khe Sanh actually increased slightly, but after an expected 2 February attack on the camp failed to materialize, the daily sortie rate was cut in half.

Although virtually all major airfields in RVN came under some form of attack, the main enemy thrusts were against Tan Son Nhut, Bien Hoa, Da Nang, and Binh Thuy. After failing to take any of the airfields, the enemy reverted (18 February) to rocket and mortar attacks. In all, 22 aircraft were destroyed and 126 damaged on the ground. The communists achieved their most dramatic success at Hue, which they held until 24 February. In the course of the month, the Citadel was reduced to rubble by airstrikes, napalm, artillery, and naval gunfire. By the end of February, the Allies had regained the initiative throughout Vietnam and were returning to the countryside.[4/]

The weight of the air response to the Tet offensive is illustrated in Figure 12. During February and March, many attack sorties were diverted from North Vietnam and STEEL TIGER and applied against the enemy in South Vietnam. The number of in-country attack sorties rose from 18,000 in January to 20,000 in February and peaked out at almost 21,000 in March. Forward Air Controllers and helicopter gunships flew constant patrols over the cities and struck against enemy holdouts. An estimated 37,000 enemy were killed in the offensive, but the psychological impact on the Allies was great. The pre-Tet confidence that the NVA was being held back at the borders of Vietnam vanished.

Whereas the VC/NVA attacks on the cities had waned by the end of February, the siege of Khe Sanh continued for another month. Lang Vei had fallen on 7 February. Early in March the siege tightened. On the first day of the month, 500 NVA troops attacked the base but were driven off by B-52s which dropped their bombs within 750 yards of the camp perimeter. Throughout March, the daily average sortie rate against troops, caves, ammunition dumps, and truck parks exceeded 300. An estimated 1,000 enemy soldiers died around Khe Sanh, compared to 200 Marines.

The last ground attack on the camp took place on 11 March; after that, the siege turned into an artillery duel. Tactical airlift kept the base alive with paradrops and use of the Low Altitude Parachute Extraction System (LAPES), which pulled cargo by parachute out the rear of the aircraft as it flew several feet above the ground. By the time Route 9 was reopened into the camp on 12 April, 1,124 airlift and 1,453 reconnaissance sorties had been flown. During the 70-day siege, 23,813 tactical strike sorties were put into the area. In the words of a Senior Army Commander, the defense of Khe Sanh was "probably the first major ground action won entirely or almost entirely by airpower."[5] A high government official viewed it as "the one decisive victory for air-power in the Vietnam war."[6] The validity of both these judgments is suggested by the preponderance of air over ground ordnance delivered during the battle:[7]

TONS OF ORDNANCE DELIVERED

By air	96,000
By Ground Artillery	3,600
TOTAL	99,600

Enemy documents captured after the battle attest to the physical and psychological impact of airstrikes on NVN soldiers. One soldier stated in his notebook that fear of B-52 raids was the main cause of desertion of 300 members of his regiment en route to the battlefield.[8] Another soldier who took part in the battle said it was much fiercer than Dien Bien Phu, and wrote:[9]

29

> *"From the beginning until the 60th day, B-52*
> *bombers continually dropped their bombs in this*
> *area with ever-growing intensity and at any moment*
> *of the day. If someone came to visit this place,*
> *he might say that this was a storm of bombs and*
> *ammunition which eradicated all living creatures*
> *and vegetation, even those located in caves or in*
> *deep underground shelters."*

Khe Sanh was an excellent example of the use of airpower in South Vietnam. In addition to troops in contact, targets during NIAGARA II included bunker storage areas and guns. The 7AF Commander coordinated and directed the tactical strikes and had his own targeting authority. The success at Khe Sanh led to a greater reliance on air and less on ground forces to interdict enemy supplies moving across the RVN borders from Laos. The enemy relied on four avenues to move his supplies into I and II Corps from STEEL TIGER: in I Corps, Routes 9/926 toward Khe Sanh, Route 922 into the A Shau Valley, and Route 165 toward Kham Duc; and in II Corps, Route 110 in the direction of Dak To. LOCs entered III and IV Corps from Cambodia (Fig. 11).

COMUSMACV summarized enemy and friendly actions during 1968 and 1969 as follows: [10/]

> *"Tet and Khe Sanh were high points for the enemy, but not*
> *for us. The whole enemy structure--Main Force, Local*
> *Force, laborers, intelligence, guides, communications,*
> *supplies--all this was at a high point of effectiveness*
> *and made it possible for him to commit his forces. How-*
> *ever, in terms of manpower, the enemy did not get hurt*
> *too badly. But he did lose quality, lose some of his*
> *experienced people. In 1968 and 1969, after Tet, we*
> *started getting into the whole enemy system with ground*
> *and air attacks, working for the attrition of the system.*
> *Such things as police activities, small unit actions,*
> *ambushes, etc., allowed for a concerted effort against*
> *the enemy's system. This caused the subsequent high*

*points not to be met or to be reduced. Due to the
effectiveness of our actions, the enemy logistical-
management system was eroded."*

The 7AF Commander agreed: [11/]

*"Khe Sanh was the beginning of the end for the communists
in their military operations in South Vietnam. And there
is no question that air was responsible for the enemy setback at Khe Sanh. During the Tet Offensive, when the
enemy got to Saigon and was not able to get the popular
uprising he hoped for and the government didn't collapse,
the result was an emotional and psychological strengthening
of the government as well as a weakening of the enemy."*

May and August Offensive, 1968

The enemy's experience during the Tet offensive led him to reassess

his strategy and tactics. Realizing that his forces could not afford

another such offensive, he believed the propaganda success could be

furthered by sustaining pressure on the Allies. The VC/NVA therefore be-

came more selective in the choice of targets, staggering his blows both

in time and place. [12/]

This strategy was carried out during the second enemy offensive

during May and June. Intelligence sources indicated the offensive was

to take place in later April, but that aggressive Free World Military

Assistance Forces (FWMAF) and RVNAF spoiling actions forced a delay. Many

enemy units were noted moving on Saigon on 3 and 4 May. The attacks be-

gan shortly thereafter, with more troops committed than in February. A

total of 27 VC/NVA battalions were scheduled to attack Saigon/Tan Son

Nhut. Of these, only elements of nine were able to enter the city, with the main fighting centered around Tan Son Nhut and in Cholon. By early June, only sporadic contact continued as the Allied troops mopped up the scattered enemy survivors. The enemy attempted some degree of coordination with attacks-by-fire (ABFs) throughout the Republic, but his offensive efforts were focused on Saigon and largely preempted.[13/]

During the May-June fighting, airpower again contributed to enemy setbacks. Total attack sorties by USAF/USMC assets under single management rose 29.4 and 53.3 percent, respectively, over the April figure. Many of the strikes were flown against the VC/NVA holed up in Saigon. The ARC LIGHT program overflew the 1,800-sortie-per-month program by completing 1,854 sorties during May, the majority of which struck enemy LOCs in western II Corps.[14/]

Enemy-initiated activity returned to a low level during the latter part of June and through July. In the first half of August, he prepared for the third in his series of "general offensives," with troop replacement and resupply activity. Beginning on 18 August, attacks by fire and ground assaults took place initially in III Corps, and spreading throughout much of Vietnam during the remainder of the month. According to intelligence sources, the attacks in outlying areas, such as at Duc Lap in western II Corps, were designed to draw Allied units to the fringes and expose the population centers to direct assault. The main objectives appeared to be Da Nang in I Corps and Tay Ninh in western III Corps, the latter to force an opening toward Saigon.[15/]

Heavy contact occurred in central I Corps from 20 August until early September. The plan for a "crushing blow" against Da Nang was prevented as the Allied forces located and destroyed the attack units. Scattered but heavy fighting also took place in western II and III Corps, with the single most prolonged assault at Duc Lap CIDG camp just inside the RVN/Cambodian Border. Before the offensive was ended in September, the enemy was unable to achieve any of his objectives; he suffered heavy casualties, as friendly ground forces and airpower blasted VC/NVA troop concentrations and captured substantial amount of war materiel. That the offensive was much less intensive than planned was seen in the fact that, as one U.S. source said, "the enemy KIA figure passed 25,000 without anyone knowing for sure whether a 'third offensive' had taken place." [16/]

In-country Interdiction

Starting immediately after Tet and continuing throughout 1968-1969, the Air Force, Navy, and Marines carried out a series of interdiction campaigns along the western border of South Vietnam where the Lao road net joined the RVN national highway system. During the first half of April 1968, 7AF tactical aircraft conducted a moderate interdiction operation in the A Shau Valley south of Khe Sanh (Projects GRAND CANYON and BUFFALO). A total of 834 missions were flown in the valley and along Route 547 leading east out of the valley. Since Free Strike Zone clearance was not granted, these operations were designated close air support rather than interdiction.

33

Later in the same month, the first Specified Strike Zones (SSZs), named Bravo and Uniform, were established near Route 14 in the vicinity of Kham Duc. Since blanket military and political clearance was obtained to frag strikes into these SSZs and to have them controlled by Forward Air Controllers, these were the first true in-country interdiction campaigns. The objective was to prevent the NVA from linking Route 966 in Laos with Route 14 in RVN.

On 12 May, the Special Forces Camp at Kham Duc was evacuated by US/ARVN forces. Although the camp was under attack by two enemy regiments, the decision to abandon it was made voluntarily. The camp had already served its purpose as a forward observation post of enemy infiltration into the coastal plain. Like Khe Sanh earlier in the year, Kham Duc could have been held, but its retention would have tied up valuable ground forces at a time when the enemy was preparing for another offensive. Airpower provided the option of retaining or abandoning the camp. When the decision was made, airpower was responsible for the successful evacuation under heavy enemy attack. While C-130s, C-123s, and Army helicopters airlifted 1,400 people from the camp, 122 USAF and 16 USMC tactical air sorties kept the enemy from overrunning the post. In addition, B-52s dropped 3,450 tons of ordnance during the three-day period (11-13 May 1968). The evacuation of Kham Duc emphasized the importance of the Single Management System. With only a few hours notice, the air resources of three services were integrated into a smooth and successful operation.[17]

34

Farther south, in the Tri-Border area where Cambodia, Laos, and South Vietnam joined, a combined Army/Air Force operation, TRUSCOTT WHITE, got under way early in April (Fig. 1). The purpose of this campaign was to use airpower and ground artillery to halt NVA construction of an extension of Route 110 into South Vietnam. Between 7 April and 29 June, ARC LIGHT strikes hit the road, while 1,420 tactical air sorties struck enemy antiaircraft emplacements. By May, road construction had stopped.

Three Specified Strike Zones were created in May around NVA LOCs in western South Vietnam: SSZ Victor in the A Shau Valley, SSZ Tango South of the valley, and SSZ Song Be, north of Bien Hoa in III Corps. SSZ Victor made the entire A Shau Valley and the surrounding mountains a Free Strike Zone where airstrikes aimed at attacking NVA troops moving through the valley from Khe Sanh. South and east of the valley, SSZ Tango straddled Route 614 (Yellow Brick Road), which ran from the valley onto the eastern coastal plain toward Da Nang. Constant pounding closed the road by August. SSZ Song Be was created in III Corps to attack enemy construction of a road from Base Area 351 toward Bien Hoa. Between 19 May and 24 October, FAC-controlled airstrikes closed the road and kept it unusable. Between the end of June and late October 1968, Seventh Air Force allocated an average of ten sorties per day to this in-country interdiction effort.[18/] The in-country interdiction program was not integrated with interdiction operations across the border in Laos to the degree desired by Seventh Air Force. Ground commanders did not grant sufficient clearances for SSZs, and the special intelligence center, which had been created at 7AF for

35

the NIAGARA campaign, was disbanded. Nevertheless, the creation of these few isolated SSZs was instrumental in blunting the enemy's second offensive in May 1968, and his third offensive in August.

The flexibility of airpower in-country was demonstrated in another way during 1968--in the defense of Special Forces Camps along the western borders of South Vietnam. A string of these Civilian Irregular Defense Group camps existed in remote areas to interdict enemy LOCs. Periodically these camps, which resembled American frontier outposts, came under attack. During 1968, COMUSMACV had successfully defended the camps with tactical aircraft and ARC LIGHT sorties. In August, the Special Forces Camp at Duc Lap in II Corps came under ground attack. The USAF flew 314 tactical air sorties and nine ARC LIGHT missions, and the enemy was driven off. Particularly impressive was the performance of the AC-47 Spooky gunships which remained constantly overhead for several nights. A total of 715 enemy were killed and the camp remained in friendly hands.

A month later, airpower saved another SF camp at Thuong Duc in I Corps, west of Da Nang. All the air assets in I Corps were mobilized to counter a sudden attack on the camp by two enemy regiments. There was a continual stream of airstrikes by USAF tactical aircraft, B-52s, and AC-47 and AC-130 gunships over Thuong Duc. In the words of the Senior U.S. Army Advisor to the Special Forces in I Corps: "There is no doubt about it. Without that support from FACs and fighters, we would not be in Thuong Duc today."[19/] The same result, along with similar laudatory comments, was experienced at several other camps before the wet season brought an end to the attacks.

Out-Country Interdiction

Route Package I: More air interdiction throughout 1968-1969 took place outside South Vietnam, in Route Package I (RP I) during the summer of 1968 and in STEEL TIGER late in 1968 and through 1969. The partial bombing halt early in April 1968 released numerous sorties from the upper Route Packages of North Vietnam and permitted them to be concentrated in the NVN panhandle. During the first week in July, an integrated air, naval, and artillery operation (THOR) was directed against NVA field artillery and AAA positions just north of the DMZ in the TALLY HO operating area. The purpose of the operation was to neutralize the AAA threat against airborne FACs and to eliminate enemy artillery threats to the USMC supply lines just south of the DMZ. A total of 2,318 strikes and reconnaissance sorties were flown, and 8,363 tons of ordnance were delivered against enemy gun positions. In one week, 126 artillery positions, 399 AAA positions, and 2 SAM sites were destroyed. As a result, the airspace in lower TALLY HO became a relatively low-threat area.[20]

One week later on 14 July 1968, an all-out interdiction campaign began in Route Package I and continued until all bombing of the north was halted on 1 November. The largest number of sorties in the history of the northern bombing campaign was flown in RP I during July and August-- more than 14,000 in July and over 13,000 in August (Fig. 12).

37

These strikes were aimed at interdicting the main routes out of RP I into Laos and forcing enemy traffic onto the coastal plain, where it became more vulnerable to air attack. Six choke points on the two main NVN roads (Routes 15 and 137) leading to Mu Gia and Ban Karai passes were bombed daily, while at night they were hit with antipersonnel ordnance to hinder repairs. Route 15 was closed nearly all the time from September through October, and Route 137 was unusable 85-90 percent of the time in October.[21/] Truck traffic dropped 50 percent on these two routes and increased only 20 percent elsewhere in RP I. In the view of the 7AF Director of Intelligence, this interdiction campaign played a major role in disrupting the enemy's logistical preparation for a third offensive in August.[22/] At the same time, it paved the way for initiation of the MACV accelerated pacification campaign aimed at the destruction of the communist infrastructure in South Vietnam. In discussing the new pacification program in January 1969, the Commander, 7AF, noted:[23/]

> "The accelerated pacification program could well be the final phase of the conflict in South Vietnam. It could not be initiated earlier because the security situation would not permit. It was initiated last fall because of the success of the air interdiction campaign in North Vietnam, which together with effective ground action in South Vietnam, rendered the majority of the North Vietnamese Army units ineffective and forced the withdrawal of many from South Vietnam."

COMMANDO HUNT: After North Vietnam was placed out of reach of U.S. airstrikes on 1 November 1968, the air interdiction campaign shifted from RP I across the Annam Mountain range to the COMMANDO HUNT area of the Lao

38

panhandle. Far from being an isolated effort, the COMMANDO HUNT campaign was tied directly to the in-country war. This connection was highlighted by the Commander, 7AF:[24/]

> *"The current air interdiction campaign in Laos could go down as one of the most significant actions of the war, and I emphasize that the North Vietnamese logistic flow through southern Laos must be reduced to a point where it cannot support offensive military actions by the communists in South Vietnam. Should the campaign fail to reach that objective, the result will be renewed military action by the communists in South Vietnam, with the objective of defeating the accelerated pacification program which is of such importance."*

Located west of the DMZ and extending from the DMZ northward to 18° N and southward to 16° N, the COMMANDO HUNT region contained the major entry ways from NVN into Laos (Nape, Mu Gia, and Ban Karai Passes) and the key exits from Laos into I Corps. The goal of the COMMANDO HUNT campaign (15 Nov 68 - 15 Apr 69) was to reduce the NVA logistical flow by increasing the time it took the enemy to move supplies into RVN and by destroying trucks and other military supplies along the routes which led into the south.[25/]

Planning: Control of the COMMANDO HUNT operations was the responsibility of the 7AF Command Center. Task Force Alpha (TFA), located at Nakhon Phanom, functioned as an Infiltration Surveillance Center (ISC) to exploit sensor information developed by the IGLOO WHITE system.

To determine the criteria for force allocation, four categories of targets were established with the following order of priority:

Type of Targets	Percent of air effort
Interdiction points	40
Truck parks and storage areas	33
Moving trucks	15-20
AAA Defenses	10- 5

Ten interdiction or Traffic Control Points (TCPs) were selected where the LOCs ran through narrow passes or along mountain sides which, when closed, forced enemy traffic to back up into truck parks and storage areas, making it a better target for airstrikes. To the destruction of truck parks and storage areas, the U.S. devoted 35 percent of its tac air and most of the B-52 strikes. Since these storage areas, unlike other types of targets, could be struck at any time of the day and in most kinds of weather, they provided alternate targets for diverted aircraft, thereby increasing the flexibility of strike planning.

Air resources were integrated for the combined truck-killing campaign against the third category of targets. The F-4s and other jets kept the trucks off the roads during the day. Defoliation thinned out the thick jungle canopy along the routes, exposing enemy trucks at night to attacks by predominantly slower-moving aircraft (A-26s, A-1s, B-57s, and AC-123/ 130 gunships). By detecting vibrations of moving trucks, IGLOO WHITE sensors provided intelligence which assisted strike, FAC, and gunship aircraft to locate the vehicles. Included in the fourth category of targets (AAA) were weapons ranging in size from 12.7-mm to 57-mm, which were located along the main route structure below Mu Gia and Ban Karai Passes and around Tchepone (Fig 10). The percentage of aircraft sent against these guns varied with the intensity of enemy AAA firing.[26/]

The Campaign: By May 1969, the COMMANDO HUNT campaign had passed through three distinct phases. Throughout the first phase, which lasted until the end of 1968, the TCPs received the major emphasis, and traffic was successfully blocked at the key interdiction points. At the same time, airstrikes against trucks, truck parks, and storage areas destroyed large quantities of enemy materiel. An average of 124 strike sorties each day and 40 each night (50 percent of the total) struck the inter-diction points. By mid-December, it was estimated from sensor informa-tion, NVA truck movement had been slowed to the point the enemy required between six and eight days to move his supplies from Mu Gia Pass into South Vietnam--a journey that had taken two to four days one year earlier. The NVA gradually adapted to the situation by building bypasses and stationing work crews near the target areas to repair the closed roads. During the last two weeks of the year, enemy truck traffic was again on the rise.[27/]

The U.S. response came during the second phase of COMMANDO HUNT, January to February 1969, when more flexibility was introduced into the operation. Target priorities were made less rigid and could be changed when necessary to counter enemy reactions. New interdiction points were established and a higher priority was given to striking stockpiles behind them. Nightly strikes on convoys and vehicles continued in an effort to reduce further the enemy's truck inventory and to funnel his traffic into more desirable strike areas. The Rules of Engagement were relaxed. Positive control areas, ten miles along the eastern border of Laos, were opened to interdiction strikes. FACs were no longer needed for attacks on TCPs. Special ARC LIGHT Operating Areas (SALOAs) were established in which multiple strikes could be made without the need for new validation for each strike. Greater reliance was placed on information derived from IGLOO WHITE sensors, which had the advantage over other intelligence sources of providing near real-time information on enemy traffic patterns, truck parks, storage areas, bypasses, and new routes. [28/]

Several of the techniques used during the second phase were refined during the final phase of the campaign (Mar-Apr 69). Important advances were made in the use of sensor information. Individual sensors were closely monitored, and interpreters were able to determine vehicle speed and predict when trucks would pass each subsequent sensor in the string. New storage areas and routes were pinpointed by the sensors. A modification was also made in the tactics used to attack interdiction points. Emphasis shifted from attacks on Traffic Control Points to attacks on Traffic Control Areas (TCAs). Special munition "packages" containing antipersonnel as well as antivehicular munitions were dropped in these areas to prevent enemy crews from moving in to repair the roads immediately after they were closed. Experiments with long-range navigation (LORAN) improved the package concept by allowing the munitions to be delivered regardless of weather conditions.29/

Results: In the five months of the campaign, 67,094 tactical air and 3,811 B-52 sorties were flown against LOCs, truck parks, storage areas, moving trucks, and AAA in STEEL TIGER--nearly all in the COMMANDO HUNT area. Tactical air alone accounted for a daily average of 46 road and bridge cuts. More than 4,300 trucks were destroyed and over 1,600 damaged. Analysts at 7AF estimated that only 18 percent of the enemy's logistical input into Laos reached South Vietnam. The remaining 82 percent was either destroyed (47 percent), consumed in the system (29 percent), or put into storage (6 percent).

The effect on the enemy's activity in RVN was dramatic. Since his Lao pipeline was plugged at the northern end, he had to supply his troops in South Vietnam from the materiel already stored in Laos. His inability to increase his stockpiles in South Vietnam prevented him from raising the level of combat activity between January and April or from maintaining the same level after the arrival of the southwest monsoon season in April. These results were achieved through a combination of interdiction attacks in the COMMANDO HUNT area and combat operations in South Vietnam.[30] Gen. Creighton Abrams, Jr., COMUSMACV, later emphasized the partnership between air interdiction and ground combat, and its success in this campaign:[31]

> "The air effort in Laos during the dry season was to
> interdict. In 1968, the program was successful. We
> know this, because when the dry season was over /the
> enemy/ didn't have enough supplies in SVN to meet his

*purpose during the wet season. He, of course,
planned for a certain amount of losses, but I
think his losses exceeded what he had planned
for his operations in upper II Corps and I Corps.
In 1968, the effort was also successful because
of a good combination of pressure on the ground,
finding the enemy's supply and making him use it
up, and the air interdiction in Laos."*

Accelerated Pacification Campaign; Pacification and Development Plan

In April 1968, COMUSMACV reviewed developments from the time the
enemy launched his Tet offensive. This review confirmed that the RVNAF
and FWMAF had achieved a significant victory in stopping the enemy and
restoring the situation. Plans called for relentless pressure on the
enemy to achieve a major turn in the course of the war and emphasized
control of population centers to deprive the enemy access to his tradi-
tional recruiting base. Captured documents revealed that continual
pressure hit at the enemy's already flagging morale. The friendly
strategy at this time was expressed by COMUSMACV who stated, "We must go
after the enemy throughout the country; we must hound him and hurt him." [32]

By the fourth quarter of 1968, certain effects of the coordinated
air and ground operations were becoming apparent. Intelligence reports
indicated the enemy was attempting to compensate for his tactical losses
by turning his efforts into a political offensive, so as to salvage at
least a political victory, [33] and to expand the VC cadre and infrastructure.
Accordingly, COMUSMACV called on each commander to enlarge his spoiling
and preemptive operations, i.e., "attacks against the enemy Main and Local
Forces, base areas, infiltration routes, LOCs, including an intensive

drive against the VC infrastructure and political apparatus aimed at eliminating them as rapidly as possible."[34/]

In essence, emphasis was placed on the elimination of the Viet Cong infrastructure (VCI) from the cities, villages, and hamlets comprising the major population areas of RVN. On the first of November 1968, the GVN, with the personal approval of President Nguyen Van Thieu, introduced a crash program to seize the military and political initiative while the enemy was in a vulnerable condition. This program was called the Acceler- ated Pacification Campaign (APC), a three-month effort expected to show results by Tet in February 1969. The APC was the "curtain-raiser" for the GVN Pacification and Development Plan which set policy guidance for 1969 and which was continued with equal emphasis into 1970. For air operations, this meant keeping attack pressure on the enemy.[35/]

Fourth Offensive

In addition to the highly successful out-country interdiction cam- paign, COMMANDO HUNT, airpower contributed to blunting the Fourth offensive through continued close air support of ground forces and in-country inter- diction. During the first week of December 1968, 7AF began a successful interdiction campaign in the A Shau Valley. Immediately afterward, a ground operation (DEWEY CANYON) led to discovery of a huge amount of enemy materiel which had backed up because the enemy was unable to move in the valley. The COMMANDO HUNT campaign and the loss of supplies in- country were the primary reasons for the low intensity of the offensive in I Corps. In III Corps, from November through January, USAF provided close air support to Army spoiling operations which weakened the enemy's subsequent attacks on Bien Hoa and Long Binh in February. It was during the Fourth offensive that sensors were introduced into South Vietnam. On 1 March, the Deployable Automatic Relay Terminal (DART I) system began operations at Bien Hoa Air Base. In September 1969, the use of sensors in-country was extended to II Corps, when DART II was deployed to Pleiku Air Base to monitor enemy movement in the Tri-Border area.

The lack of aggressiveness displayed by the VC/NVA during the post-Tet 1969 offensive was testimony to the cumulative effect which years of bombing and artillery fire had upon the enemy. The enemy attacks which began on the night of 22-23 February 1969 were numerous and country-wide, but for the most part they were hit-and-run fire attacks--rocket and mortar firings against military installations. With these attacks, the enemy sought to inflict as much damage as he could with the least risk to his own forces, reversing his tactics of the preceding year when losses were subordinated to psychological impact. The cautious nature of enemy tactics was an indication of the degree to which he had been hurt during the first three offensives.

The enemy continued to build and repair his LOCs from Laos and Cambodia into RVN throughout 1969, and air attacks continued to interdict them. New Specified Strike Zones were created to correspond to the new LOCs in SSZs Sierra, Tango, Yankee, and Whiskey. Aircraft had a blanket authority to cut roads and create landslides along the routes leading into I Corps. In II Corps, SSZ Zulu was created to interdict Routes 613 and 615. Because of the presence of friendly ground forces in the A Shau Valley and around Bien Hoa, the strike zones in the valley and near Song Be were discontinued.[36/]

Sortie Reduction

The U.S. policy of de-escalation, which began with the two bombing halts of 1968, was continued in 1969 under the new administration in Washington. Vietnamization and troop redeployment were announced in mid-year. The first effect of this cutback on air resources came on 26 August 1969 when the daily in-country rate for preplanned sorties was reduced by 17 percent--from 243 to 200 sorties per day. The daily total of in-country sorties dropped from 583 to 503.[37/] At the same time, the monthly ARC LIGHT sortie rate was reduced from 1,600 to 1,400, where it remained for the rest of the year.[38/] A further cutback took place on 1 September when USAF attack sorties were limited to 14,000 per month, but the reduction in sorties was not necessarily equivalent to a reduction in effectiveness. According to a COMUSMACV statement which accompanied the cutback:[39/]

> "The number of aircraft fragged for operations in each CTZ is dependent on where the greatest enemy threat exists at a given time and the necessity to use airpower with flexibility to counter that threat. Available assets will continue to be allocated in such a way as to counter the areas of greatest enemy threat throughout the entire RVN."

47

CHAPTER IV

ELEMENTS OF THE AIR WAR

New Aircraft and Modifications

The first six OV-10 Broncos, designed for use by the FACs,[1] were deployed to SEA in July 1968 under the code name COMBAT BRONCO. They were attached to the 19th Tactical Air Support Squadron (TASS), under control of the III Direct Air Support Center (DASC), and were flown from forward operating locations throughout III CTZ.[2] The evaluation was completed on 30 October 1968 and OV-10s were deployed to the I, II, and III CTZs, as well as in Thailand.[3] In-country use was varied. The OV-10 provided its own flare light to assist in its primary functions of visual reconnaissance and tactical strike control.[4] In April 1969, a test of the OV-10 in an armed FAC role was started as Project MISTY BRONCO.[5] As a result of the program, the arming of all OV-10s was authorized on 5 June,[6] and by the end of the year, the arming program was in high gear.[7]

There were several significant modifications of existing in-theatre aircraft. The newest of the attack aircraft in South Vietnam was the B model of the A-37, which became operational in December 1969.[8] This model had equipment for in-flight refueling and a modified wing, which enabled it to operate at heavier gross weights and take a 6G stress, as compared with 5Gs for the A-37A.[9]

The workhorse of the fighters, the F-4, arrived in still another configuration in November 1968.[10] The F-4E featured higher thrust J79-17

48

engines and an internally mounted 20-mm gun.[11]

A major modification was made on the C-123 Provider with the addition of two jet engines to augment its reciprocating power. This program began in 1967, and by May 1969, all C-123s in SEA had been modified into the new model, the C-123K.[12]

Gunships

At the beginning of 1968, the fixed-wing, side-firing gunship force in SEA consisted of 32 AC-47 Spooky aircraft,[13] and one AC-130 Spectre was undergoing combat evaluation.[14] By the end of 1969, the SEA gunship force was authorized 71 aircraft with 61 assigned, including 15 AC-47s for the VNAF.[15] In South Vietnam, the dispersed basing of the gunships permitted a high degree of responsiveness to requirements of the four Corps areas. The following statistics show disposition of one SEA gunship force in late 1969:[16]

DISTRIBUTION OF GUNSHIP AIRCRAFT IN SEA
NOVEMBER 1969

Base	AC-47	AC-119G	AC-119K	AC-130A
Da Nang	4		6	
Pleiku	3			
Phu Cat			6	
Tuy Hoa		7		

Base	AC-47	AC-119G	AC-119K	AC-130A
Phan Rang	4	5	6	
Bien Hoa	3			
Tan Son Nhut	15*	5		
Ubon				6
Udorn	3**			

Throughout 1968 and 1969, the AC-47 continued to be used primarily in base and hamlet defense and in support of troops-in-contact.[17] The AC-119G Shadow G, with equipment similar to the Spooky, was introduced into SEA in December 1968. In South Vietnam, it was used predominately as an armed reconnaissance gunship.[18] Like the Spooky, the Shadow G could not operate in marginal weather, but its added firepower, its night observation device (NOD), and its illuminator and fire control system gave it greater capability and flexibility. Under visual flight conditions, it was capable of offset firing.[19] Through the computerized fire control system, the NOD was able to lock on a point and direct fire at that point or any nearby target, using the point as a reference.[20]

In October 1969, the AC-119K, known as the Stinger, was assigned to bases in South Vietnam. Its primary role was interdiction in both

* VNAF aircraft.
** TDY aircraft from among RVN bases.

Tactical Airlift at Khe Sanh
FIGURE 19

Vietnam and Laos. The Stinger's performance far exceeded that of its sister gunship, the Shadow G. Two jets augmented its reciprocating engines and an infrared detector and beacon tracking radar were tied to the fire control system in the same manner as the NOD on the Shadow G, thus giving an all-weather attack capability that included offset.[21/]

The first AC-130A squadron was activated in August 1968. Combat evaluation made it clear that the sophisticated Spectre was a very effective night interdiction weapon, particularly as a truck killer. As a result, the squadron was used mainly in the out-country interdiction campaign in Laos.[22/] The Spectre squadron was organized as part of the 8th Tactical Fighter Wing and permanently based in Thailand. All other gunships were under the 14th Special Operations Wing with home stations in RVN.[23/]

In December 1969, a specially equipped AC-130A with two 20-mm and two 40-mm guns joined the Spectre fleet under Project SURPRISE PACKAGE (Fig. 19). This aircraft was the most sophisticated of the gunships and was equipped with the following special features: S-band ignition system detection, Low-Light-Level television (LLLTV), ground moving target indicator (GMTI) radar, electro-optical sensor capability for truck and AAA detection, LORAN, an inertial navigation system interfaced with a computer to store targets of opportunity instantly, a laser target designator and ranger for use with PAVE WAY equipped F-4Ds, a digital fire control system computer, and an improved analog fire control

51

system computer. The SURPRISE PACKAGE could detect, track, and destroy trucks, petroleum storage areas, and AAA guns from an operating altitude of 12,000 feet AGL. It was able to mark targets for its escort fighters both with gunfire, laser, and LORAN coordinates, perform as a HUNTER-KILLER, and use real-time sensor information from TFA by virtue of its secure voice capability.[24] The Secretary of the Air Force, Dr. Robert C. Seamans, Jr., indicated the value of the weapons system when he said that he believed there was no more important use for the C-130 airframe than the gunship role, especially when configured as SURPRISE PACKAGE.[25] He further proposed that the other AC-130s be converted to the SURPRISE PACKAGE configuration as soon as possible.[26] As of 22 January 1970, gunships were accounting for 39 percent of all trucks destroyed and damaged in the interdiction campaign. The SURPRISE PACKAGE was well ahead of the other gunships, averaging 5.54 trucks destroyed or damaged per sortie, compared with 2.52 for the Spectre and .36 for tactical fighters.[27]

The VNAF became an integral part of the SEA gunship force, activating its first AC-47 squadron in July 1969.[28] The VNAF gunships provided firepower for base defense and support of ARVN operations, particularly in IV CTZ.[29] A second VNAF AC-47 squadron was programmed for activation at Da Nang in the first quarter of FY 72.[30]

The mixed gunship force was multi-mission capable. In the five years of its operation, it provided base defense, fire support for

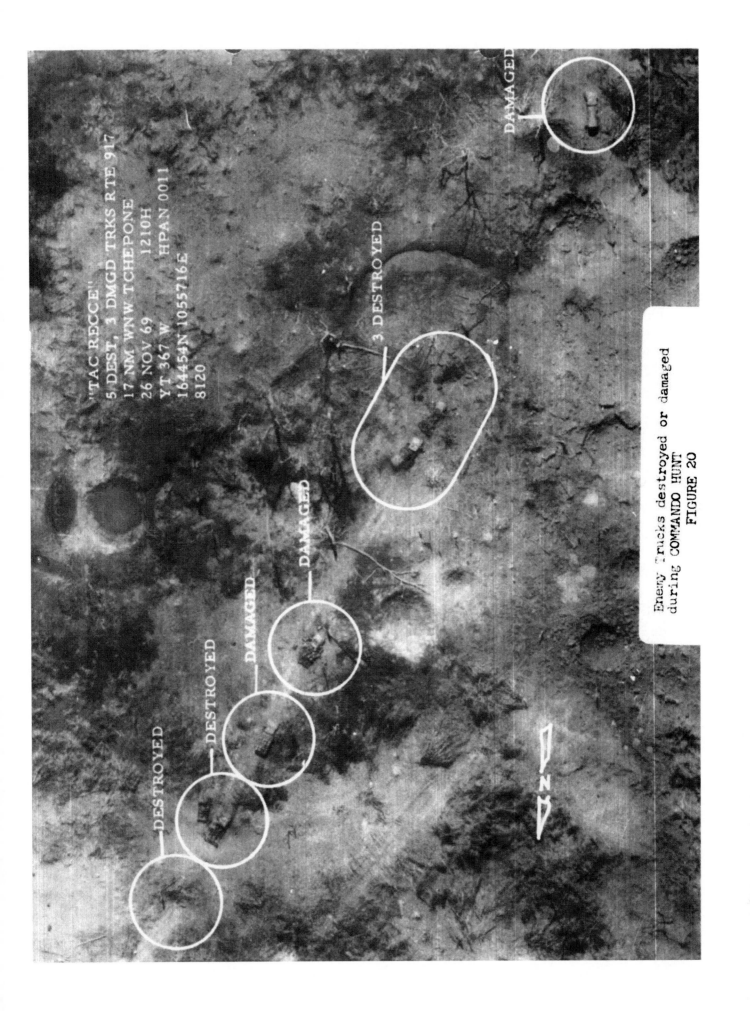

"TAC RECCE"
5 DEST, 3 DMGD TRKS R TE 917
17 NM WNW TCHEPONE
26 NOV 69   1210H
YT 367 W   HPAN 0011
164454N 1055716E
8120

DESTROYED

DESTROYED

DAMAGED

DAMAGED

3 DESTROYED

DAMAGED

Enemy Trucks destroyed or damaged
during COMMANDO HUNT
FIGURE 20

F-4 Phantom Jets and KC-135 Stratotanker
FIGURE 21

40-mm Cannon used on AC-130
Spectre Gunship
FIGURE 22

troops-in-contact, and interdiction. [31/] Support of Special Forces Camps

and troops-in-contact was the most frequent application.

New Weapons

There were a number of new and improved weapons introduced into the

war during 1968 and 1969. Three missiles were introduced in 1968--the

AIM-9E, an air-to-air missile with improved maneuverability, the AIM-7E/

2, an improved version of the Sparrow missile, and the AGM-78A, an

improved air-to-ground missile particularly suited for use against SAM

sites. [32/]

The PAVE WAY I, laser guided bomb, was tested, found operationally

suitable, and incorporated into the inventory. It was followed in early

1969 by PAVE WAY II, with an electro-optical guidance system which was

designed for extreme accuracy. [33/]

The munitions available for the 1969-1970 Northeast Monsoon Cam-

paign, COMMANDO HUNT III, formed the most versatile mix ever available

to Seventh Air Force. [34/] These included a number of long-established

weapons as well as the more specialized PAVE WAY and WALLEYE guided

bombs, the FMU-72 fuse, and the M-36 incendiary cluster. The ROCKEYE II

armor piercing munition was introduced in October 1969 as a flak sup-

pressant and truck killer. The WALLEYE electro-optically guided bomb

became operational in early 1968 and was found to be very accurate. [35/]

The FMU-72 fuse was a variable time delay fuse with random delay settings

up to 144 hours. It was especially effective when seeded concurrently with MK-36 mines. The M-36 incendiary cluster was particularly effective against trucks. The BLU-31/B, designed for cratering heavily fortified structures, and the 15,000-pound BLU-82B were tested for use in clearing large helicopter landing zones in forested areas.[36/]

To improve efficiency of munitions in theater, the Directorate of Air Munitions, Seventh Air Force, completed a study in March 1969 of the proliferation of munition types. The objective was to limit as much as possible redundant munitions and to eliminate those which had outlived their usefulness, so as to reduce system complexity.[37/] By the end of 1969, substantial progress had been made.

Support of Special Forces Camps

Special Forces Camps (also referred to as CIDG camps) were placed in a line running roughly north and south the length of Vietnam, mostly near the western border area.[38/] The strength of each camp was about 600--a majority of the force being Civilian Irregular Defense Group personnel, along with a small number of U.S. Special Forces Advisors.[39/] The isolated nature of these camps made them vulnerable to attack and also extraordinarily dependent upon airpower for fire and logistic support.

The organization of this support was spelled out in 7AF Operations Plan 443-69, which provided for camp defense and evacuation, if needed. A number of agencies were involved in the process. The key to the orderly functioning of defense of CIDG camps was the Direct Air Support

Special Forces Bivouac in Quang Ngai
Province

FIGURE 47

Center (DASC) in whose area the site was located. The DASC was responsible for coordination of the total air effort in support of the camps,
as well as other air support within its area of operation.[40/]

The forward point of SF Camp defense was the FAC who, in many
cases, lived with the Army and was most familiar with the SF Camp, its
method of operation, terrain, defenses, and other vital information.
He was also the airborne element of the defense force in radio contact
with the SF Camp which had the most timely information on the situation
during an attack.[41/]

Each Tactical Fighter Wing was assigned a number of SF Camps to support. These wings maintained special folders on each camp and kept all
pilots current on camp status, possible primary targets, terrain, and
other features. In addition, each pilot was required to overfly the
assigned camps periodically and to remain current on landmarks, flight
routes, and defense procedures.[42/]

When CIDG camps found themselves under heavy attack, such as at
Kham Duc in May 1968, the Tactical Air Control Center worked closely
with the Airlift Control Center and SAC units to insure that enough
airlift, B-52s, and refueling resources were available. Fighter aircraft were diverted from their preplanned missions and scrambled as they
were needed. All tactical airpower on the scene was controlled by the
ABCCC, which coordinated closely with DASC, the Tactical Air Control

Party, and the ALO to insure a smooth flow of all types of aircraft.
Army resources were integrated by close coordination with Army CH-47
helicopter control aircraft and ground elements on the scene. As much
of the total airpower in Southeast Asia as necessary was available for
CIDG camp emergencies.[43/]

In the enemy's early 1968 onslaught, he was able to take Lang Vei
and Kham Duc SF Camps. From that time through early 1970, however, none
had been lost, although the enemy, apparently incapable of large scale
attacks, continued his efforts against SF Camps (Bien Het, Phu Duc, Bu
Prang, and others).[44/]

Tactical airlift was also a vital part of SF Camp support. During
the last half of 1968, for example, more than 84 percent of the camp's
logistical support was by airlift.[45/]   This support was the responsibility
of the 834th Air Division, which provided not only aircraft but also
combat control teams for on-site traffic control, mobility teams for
rapid on-load capability, and aircraft maintenance teams. The resources
used were varied, depending upon size and capability of the landing strip
at the SF Camp. A majority of the sites were supplied by the C-7, since
it could operate from 1,000-foot runways. Resupply by airdrop was
vital in combat situations.[46/]

Tactical Airlift

The C-130, C-123, and C-7A aircraft were used in tactical airlift
operations.[47/]   The C-130 operated in-country on rotational TDY from the

56

Airdrop Resupply by C-130 Hercules
FIGURE 24

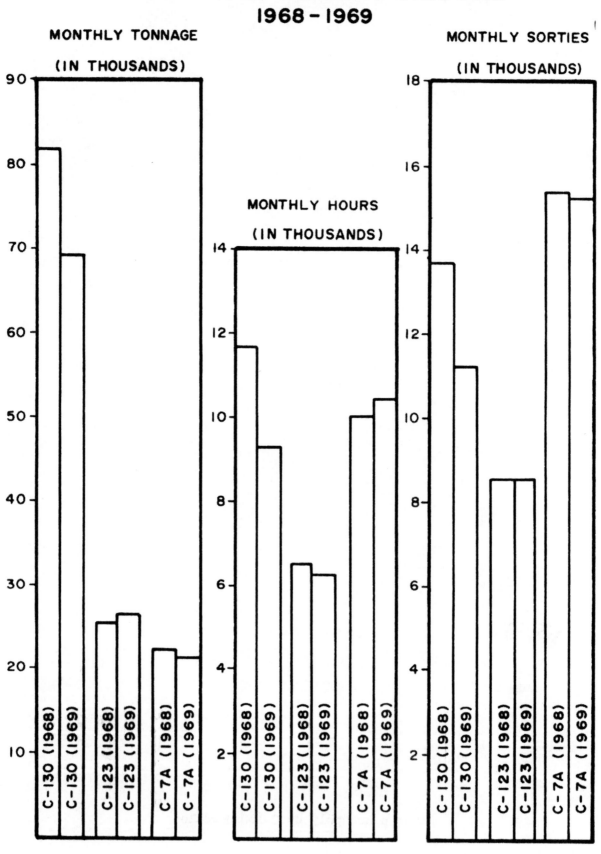

FIGURE 25

Philippines, Taiwan, Okinawa, and Japan, while the C-123s and C-7s were based in Vietnam.[48/] Nearly all cargo and passengers were carried by the C-130; the C-7A was used in short fields because of its short takeoff and landing (STOL) characteristics;[49/] and a number of C-7As were dedicated to specific Army units.[50/]

All of the tactical airlift in-country was controlled by the 834th Air Division, including the TDY C-130s. Airlift requirements were forwarded from users to MACV Traffic Management Agency (TMA), which levied requirements on the 834th.[51/] Certain mission priorities took precedence over scheduled flights, including tactical emergencies (actual or imminent contact with the enemy), emergency resupply, combat essential missions, and urgent medical evacuation.[52/]

In 1968, the tactical airlift force hauled a total of 130,000 tons on 38,000 sorties with 28,000 hours of flying time per month. The figures for 1969 were 112,000 tons, 34,700 sorties, and 25,700 hours. (Figure 25 lists tonnage, flying hours, and sorties by aircraft.) During two periods of high activity in 1968--February and March, October and November--the airlift force was augmented by the use of UC-123 (spray) aircraft in a cargo hauling configuration.[53/] The performance of the C-123 was considerably enhanced during 1968-1969 by the addition of two jet engines.[54/]

Special crisis situations graphically illustrate the critical nature of tactical airlift. In the 1968 siege of Khe Sanh, for instance, without tactical airlift, the base would have been completely isolated. Within the three-month period, January-March 1968, the 834th Air Division delivered 12,400 tons of supplies both by airdrop and by landing under extremely hazardous conditions. In addition, wounded personnel were evacuated by airlift. New tactics, such as radar-vectored supply drops during Instrument Flight Rules (IFR) conditions were also perfected.[55]

Tactical airlift in SEA steadily became more efficient. It was absolutely essential to the support of the CIDG, to all the four Corps Tactical Zones, and to the movement of ammunition, POL, and people.[56] General Brown, Commander, 7AF, spoke of tactical airlift as "critical to everything that goes on in this war."[57]

All-Weather and Night Operations

Operations at night and in bad weather conditions were critical roles of tactical air support in Southeast Asia.[58] To overcome the operational problems, three approaches were in use in Vietnam at the end of 1969: artificial light, COMBAT SKYSPOT, and the Marine's A-6A Diane system.[59]

Two basic types of artificial light were available. The primary sources were flares of various kinds, dropped either by flares or gunships, by the lead fighter in a flight, or in rare cases, by the FAC himself. Both the F-100 and the F-4 had flares on the lead aircraft standing night alert. The A-37 had not been modified for this mission at the end of 1969, but a study was under way to determine its

58

feasibility.[60/] The OV-10 and O-2 FACs were used to drop flares on occasion.[61/] The O-1 did not have this capability. The second type of light was the illuminator on the AC-119K.

This system was designed to improve visibility and target acquisition for use in close air support at night. It was not widely used because illuminators were on the AC-119K, operating out-country in a night truck killing role. In this role, the illuminator was not required. Operating with artificial light, the delivery parameters were generally the same as during daylight. Using the illuminator along LOCs would have highlighted the aircraft, making it extremely vulnerable to ground fire.[62/]

MSQ-77 radar, called COMBAT SKYSPOT, was the primary means of weather delivery and was also widely used at night. The Air Force required that COMBAT SKYSPOT drops be no closer than 1,000 meters to friendly troops. MSQ-77 radar sites were located throughout Southeast Asia and gave coverage to all of South Vietnam, except for a small portion of II CTZ. The operator would vector the aircraft to the target and provide a countdown for weapon release based on his radar presentation.[63/] A system similar to the COMBAT SKYSPOT operation was used by Marine aircraft in I CTZ; it used the same procedures, but the radar facilities were compatible only to Marine aircraft.[64/]

The Marine A-6S in I CTZ also had a bombing system called Diane, consisting of an airborne radar set, a mobile ground beacon, and a ground

59

located FAC. By using a known beacon location, the offset distance and bearing to the target were determined by the FAC and programmed into the aircraft's bombing computer. The radar operator could then use the beacon impulse as a radar target while the aircraft made its bomb run on the offset target up to 99,999 feet away. Using the Diane system, drops as close as 500 meters to friendly troops were allowed.[65/]

Weather minimums for visual bombing and support of TICs varied not only with aircraft type but also with terrain, troop situations, and ordnance carried. Generally, minimums ranged from a ceiling of 300 feet and 2 miles visibility for the A-1 to 1,500 feet and 5 miles for the F-4 and F-100. Lower weather conditions required the use of the all-weather procedures and equipment described previously.[66/]

Two other night and all-weather systems or procedures, LORAN and COMMANDO NAIL, were used in Laos but not in South Vietnam.[67/] The former capability was provided only on certain F-4s at Ubon RTAFB, while the latter used the airborne computer system on the F-4.

ARC LIGHT missions used two methods of ordnance delivery. About 95 percent of the time they used COMBAT SKYSPOT. The highly accurate, self-contained radar bombing system of the B-52 was occasionally used to bomb primary targets and a majority of the secondary targets.[68/]

Electronic Warfare and Reconnaissance

Electronic warfare and reconnaissance were performed by two aircraft, the EB-66 and the EC-47. The former was primarily an electronic counter-measure (ECM) aircraft while the latter contained extensive Airborne

EB-66 Aircraft,
FIGURE 26

Radio Direction Finding (ARDF) equipment. In addition, there were several other resources used out-country.

The Army OV-1 Mohawk was deployed in B and C Model configuration. The B Model was equipped with Side-Looking Airborne Radar (SLAR) and Moving Target Indicator (MTI) systems. The C model had infrared detection gear. These aircraft gave near-real-time readout of operational intelligence in the cockpit. The Navy RA-5C was equipped with an infrared mapping system and SLAR. It also carried its own ECM equipment for self-protection. Strategic intelligence was gathered by high flying U-2s and SR-71s, while the SC-147 drones were effective intelligence vehicles over heavily defended areas of NVN. [69]

The activities of the EB-66 were many and varied. It provided ECM and threat warning for B-52 missions. It was used to identify, locate, and analyze the technical parameters of hostile radar environment. In 1969, the aircraft was equipped with a directional antenna system which was very effective in drone support. Another function of the EB-66 was detection of enemy Fan Song missile guidance signals. In early 1969, there were 38 EB-66s in Southeast Asia, but the 41st Tactical Electronic Warfare Squadron (TEWS) was deactivated in October 1969 and the EB-66s in theater were reduced to 20. Several improvements in the electronic capability of the aircraft had been forecast, but they, too, were eliminated by the fiscal austerity of 1969. [70] Activity was also curtailed by engine problems from April through June 1969. [71] Nonetheless, the EB-66 was still the primary ECM aircraft in Southeast Asia at the end of 1969.

The C-47 continued to add to its long list of accomplishments in Southeast Asia in its role as an ARDF platform in the EC-47 configuration. In 1968, a project known as COMBAT COUGAR[72/] was designed to satisfy the Field Force Commander's requests for ARDF to locate enemy transmitters.[73/] The information was passed by secure voice to Army Direct Support units as soon as possible.[74/] EC-47 operations were extensive, with 2,485 in-country missions flown in the fourth quarter of 1968.[75/] Plans at the beginning of 1969 called for an increase from 49 to 57 aircraft. The general austerity of 1969 did not affect the EC-47 program which, because of its low cost and overall success, was expanded. Frequency coverage was increased and by the end of the year, 6 aircraft had been sent to Nakhon Phanom RTAFB under Operation COMMANDO FORGE for use out-country.[76/]

In addition to the ECM function of the EB-66, there was a continuing need for integral ECM capabilities on fighter aircraft. Both the F-4 and F-105 were equipped with warning receivers against SAM and AAA threats in addition to ECM pods. Warning equipment was also installed in about 75 percent of the F-100s in theater. The VHF jammers were programmed for the F-105 but further testing and development were required.[77/]

At the beginning of 1969, only a limited number of 7AF tactical aircraft and approximately 50 percent of the ground control facilities were equipped for secure voice operations. The continued implementation of Tactical Secure Voice (TSV) was hampered by lack of modifications in F-4 and F-105 aircraft. Progress was made, however, and by the end of the year, about 600 aircraft, one-third of the total assigned, were equipped with TSV. Approximately 90 percent of the modification of ground facilities was completed.[78/]

There was still a definite requirement for electronic warfare and intelligence at the end of 1969, given the improvement of the NVN defense posture and the possibility of radar controlled defenses in Laos. COMUSMACV considered intelligence acquisition from all sources--human and man-made--a command responsibility equal to the employment of combat power.[79/]

Air Defense

There were three major components in the air defense system in South Vietnam: various radar sites throughout the country, the Tactical Air Control Centers, and the interceptor aircraft on alert at Da Nang and Chu Lai. With only minor changes, the system remained the same during 1968 and 1969.[80/]

For the purposes of air defense, South Vietnam was divided into two sectors, with the focal point at the respective TACCs. The North Sector (NS) TACC, code name MOTEL, was located at Da Nang, with responsibility for the area north of Pleiku.[81/] MOTEL was a computerized TACC

63

which compiled radar information from various sources to monitor air traffic in North Vietnam: Navy (Red Crown), Marine (Vice Squad), EC-121 (COLLEGE EYE), and Air Force (Panama at Da Nang, RVN, and Brigham at Udorn, Thailand). The key to the operation was SEEK DAWN, a project which employed computer data link to integrate the basically incompatible Navy and Air Force radar.[82/] Vital information gathered at TACC (NS) was also passed by communications line to the TACC at Tan Son Nhut, which was the primary TACC for Vietnam and also responsible for air defense from Pleiku south. Both TACCs received inputs from the various radar sites throughout South Vietnam through the two main Control and Reporting Centers (CRCs) at Da Nang (Panama) and Tan Son Nhut (Paris). The activity of MIGs in the North was also monitored and evaluated for any significant movement which might change the alert posture.[83/]

Primary air defense resources available to the TACCs were four F-4Es at Da Nang (Gunfighter) and two Marine F-4s at Chu Lai (Love Bug). Two of the Da Nang aircraft were on five-minute alert and the other two on one hour alert. The Marine aircraft were on 15 minute alert. The latter were also the primary MIGCAP aircraft. If more resources were needed for air defense, it was planned to obtain them from tactical fighter squadrons. Prior to 15 November 1969, the primary air defense aircraft at Da Nang were six F-102s. On that date, the F-4E replaced the F-102 and the number of alert aircraft was reduced from six to four. There were no specific aircraft committed to air defense against possible intrusion from Cambodia.[84/]

A majority of air defense scrambles were to identify unknown aircraft or to provide MIGCAP during such activities as search and rescue (SAR) efforts. On 5 December 1969, for example, two F-4s were scrambled from Da Nang since MIG radio calls indicated a possible threat to a SAR effort in progress.[85/] An example of another type of air defense situation occurred in June 1968, when a number of enemy helicopters were detected moving from the DMZ to Tiger Island. The normal air defense system was augmented, in that case, by laser range finders and night observation devices under Operation HAVE FEAR. Although several helicopters were attacked, the results were not known.[86/]

At the end of 1969, there was no VNAF air defense system nor were there any VNAF aircraft standing alert. VNAF assets were used by the USAF system on occasion, particularly against possible intrusions from Cambodia.[87/]

A primary responsibility of the air defense system by late 1969 was monitoring ARC LIGHT strikes for SAM, AAA, and MIG locations and threats. If support or escort aircraft were needed, they were made available by the TACC.[88/]

ARC LIGHT

The B-52 operations in Southeast Asia (ARC LIGHT)[89/] were being flown at the rate of 800 sorties per month at the beginning of 1968 from Andersen AFB, Guam, and U-Tapao RTAB, Thailand.[90/] On 1 February, the sortie rate was increased to 1,200 and to 1,800 on 15 February because of the Pueblo crisis and the siege of Khe Sanh.   Kadena AFB, Okinawa, was added as a base of operations on the latter date.[91/]   The 1,800 sortie rate continued until October 1969 when the rate was reduced to 1,400 sorties per month.[92/]   The standard bomb load for sorties throughout the period was twenty-four 500-pound bombs carried externally and eighty-four internally (27 tons) for U-Tapao aircraft, and twenty-four 500-pound bombs externally and forty-two 750-pound bombs internally for Kadena and Andersen aircraft (23 tons).[93/]

Khe Sanh proved to be a watershed for B-52 operations in SEA.   As a result of this siege, the sortie rate was increased to 1,800 per month and close-in bombing (within 1,000 meters of friendly forces) was inaugurated as a direct close air support tactic.   Another innovation was BUGLE NOTE.   Prior to the siege, the most rapid response was a seven-hour ground divert capability from U-Tapao.[94/]   The BUGLE NOTE concept fragged a cell of three B-52s to a given pre-Initial Point (IP) every one and a half hours to be targeted from that point by MSQ radar. BUGLE NOTE permitted target changes as late as one and a half hours prior to the scheduled time over target (TOT).   The force allocation was later changed to a six-aircraft cell every three hours over the pre-IP, with a selective target change three hours before TOT.[95/]

The results of B-52 strikes were difficult to evaluate in terms of BDA but the psychological impact was immense.   The PWs and Hoi Chanhs indicated airstrikes forced them to move constantly, kept them off balance, caused numerous casualties, lowered morale, and prevented them

B-52s in Action
FIGURE 27

from staging significant offensive action.[96/]   As a result, on 1 April
1969, one B-52 in each three-ship cell began to carry one MI29RI leaflet bomb to drop with the strike, exploiting the psychological impact.[97/]
A single B-52 mission, consisting normally of six aircraft, could
deliver approximately 150 tons of ordnance on a two-kilometer square
target with better than 99 percent accuracy. For tactical fighters to
deliver the same tonnage would require many times that number of aircraft.[98/]

The B-52 target nominations were made by field commanders, COMUSMACV,
and Seventh Air Force. Target approval rested with MACV. Each Field
Force or other nominating agency was responsible for assuring the military
and political clearance of each target. The final determination of
targets for ARC LIGHT strikes was usually made by the Deputy J-3 for
Operations at MACV. While a number of the aircraft were fragged for
preplanned targets, all operated under the BUGLE NOTE system.[99/]

U.S. commanders were so concerned about getting more B-52 strikes
in their area of operations that they often went to great lengths to
request such support. At one point, for example, General Corcoran,
First Field Force Commander, made a special trip to COMUSMACV during
particularly heavy fighting in his area (October 1969) to make a personal plea for more ARC LIGHT support.[100/]   The power of this weapon
was clearly recognized by every U.S. commander from General Abrams on
down. His statement on ARC LIGHT in the fall of 1968 demonstrated this
enthusiasm:[101/]

"In one instance where no ground forces were available (NW Kontum Province), the enemy was stopped by repeated B-52 strikes alone. Every time the enemy is found massing anywhere within South Vietnam, he is hit in this way. The B-52 used in this manner under centralized control becomes a tool of such effectiveness that the theater commander has no possible substitute within the conventional arsenal. Without B-52 sorties, the theater commander would need more ground troops to achieve the results obtained since initiation of this B-52 concept. This concept has been so effective that ground commanders' requests for B-52 strikes continue to exceed available sorties.

"In summary, the B-52s are the theater commander's reserve, his artillery, his interdiction tool, his means for influencing the battle, and in some instances his only means for meeting the enemy immediately upon discovery."

Use of Sensors

In South Vietnam, the primary function of tactical air continued to be response to the daily close air support requirements of ground commanders, including special air operations in support of Special Forces Camps. The interdiction role still maintained its significance, however, especially during the months of the dry Northeast Monsoon. Critical to the role of interdiction, especially in the Specified Strike Zones, were sensors.[102/] The use of sensors of various types on a reasonably large scale in South Vietnam can be dated from the battle of Khe Sanh during the first three months of 1968. During that engagement large numbers of air-delivered electronic sensors were implanted to detect enemy movements. This use attracted a great deal of interest both in the concept and in sensor reliability.[103/] Artillery was pre-aimed on sensor strings and fired when activations occurred, with very

68

satisfactory results.[104/]

In the months that followed Khe Sanh, the use of sensors in the DMZ and I CTZ was expanded (DUEL BLADE).[105/] In addition, plans were formulated to use sensors in other parts of Vietnam in support of ground operations in antiinfiltration technology,[106/] and to provide near real-time intelligence information on personnel and vehicular positions and movements (DUFFEL BAG).[107/]

Both seismic and acoustic sensors were used. Acoubuoy and Spike-buoy were acoustic; Adsid, Helosid, and Handsid were seismic. In addition, other more specialized sensors were used, such as, the Magid, which detected metallic objects, and the Pirid, which used infrared technology.[108/] Sensor impulses were either read directly through hand monitoring devices or were picked up by an orbiting EC-121 and then relayed to the readout facility, either at Nakhon Phanom RTAFB or the Army and Marine facilities in I CTZ.

Aside from the use of sensors in I CTZ and the DMZ, their use in South Vietnam centered around the Deployable Automatic Relay Terminal (DART) facilities at Bien Hoa (DART I) and Pleiku (DART II). The DARTs were complete sensor readout and interpretation facilities which provided near-real-time (less than one minute) sensor interpretation to Army units for artillery fire and LOC surveillance.[109/] DART I became operational on 1 March 1969. Because of the level terrain of the Mekong Delta region, data were relayed to this facility through an Automatic Data

Relay atop Mui Ba Den Mountain. The data from DART II, which began
operation on 28 September 1969, were relayed through orbiting EC-121 aircraft. DART II was also used as a training facility for VNAF personnel
who were to be integrated into the operation of the system.[110/]

At the end of 1969, approximately 560 IGLOO WHITE sensors were being
monitored by Air Force facilities in support of COMMANDO HUNT III, with
65 strings in STEEL TIGER, 4 strings in BARREL ROLL, and 15 strings in
DUEL BLADE/I CTZ. Delivery of Phase III sensors and other components
was expected during 1970. Whether they would be used in-country was
undecided.[111/]

In addition to these electronic sensors, a number of other sensor-
surveillance techniques and instruments were being employed in Vietnam.
Airborne infrared sensors were used to detect personnel and vehicles
by heat indications. Side-Looking Airborne Radar and Side-Looking Infrared Radar detected moving vehicles, boats, and groups of people. Ground
surveillance radar was able to observe ground movements within its
field of coverage. Night observation devices (NODs) and Starlight
Scopes enabled the user to see movement and targets by amplifying available night light. Data from all of these sources, plus visual reconnaissance, photo reconnaissance, and intelligence reports were combined
to provide timely information on enemy locations, assets, and movements.[112/]

Herbicide Operations

At the beginning of 1968, there were 17 UC-123 RANCH HAND aircraft

70

available to perform the dual herbicide missions of removing natural cover to expose enemy positions and destroy enemy crops.[113] By late 1969, this number had been increased to 25 and all had been converted to K models (jet engines added).[114]

Operations in 1968 were curtailed by the use of the aircraft as cargo haulers during Tet and again in October and November.[115] During the period from 1 January 1968 through 30 June 1969, RANCH HAND aircraft dispensed about 7,500,000 gallons of herbicide on approximately 2,500,000 acres.[116] Average monthly sorties for 1968 were 443 and for 1969, 450. Of special importance were activities in I CTZ where several LOCs near Da Nang and Phu Bai were defoliated.[117] Crop destruction was particularly effective in areas of I and II CTZ where the enemy had to exist far removed from population centers. Aircraft remained at Da Nang throughout 1969 to continue this effort.[118]

Vulnerability to ground fire remained a problem in 1968-1969 and was inherent in the slow speed, low altitude requirement for spraying. As a result, the possibility of employing jet aircraft in the defoliation role was explored, and the first F-4 spray mission was flown on 26 January 1969 in Laos. Limited out-country application continued.[119] In addition, all herbicide missions employed a fighter escort of at least two aircraft.[120] The practice of using a FAC for all spray missions was also adopted in 1968.[121] Weather conditions were a big factor in mission completion because certain temperatures, humidity, and wind conditions were necessary for maximum effectiveness. Finally,

71

the excessive time required to obtain clearance for a herbicide operation remained. All defoliation projects required U.S. Embassy and RVNAF Joint General Staff approval. The time delay was sometimes as much as two and one-half months.[122/]

RANCH HAND aircraft were also active in the out-country war, defoliating key LOCs and suspected supply dumps. The use of the C-130 to dispense barrels of flammable material to be ignited by grenades or rocket was explored both as a defoliation and an antipersonnel/anti-vehicle weapon.[123/] It was quite apparent that the enemy's food supply, his ability to travel undetected, and the number of hiding places he had available were adversely affected by the defoliation effort.[124/] As 1969 drew to a close, however, the defoliation role was declining in importance as the Free World Forces began to move into enemy areas and supply lines.[125/]

Air Base Defense

The battalion-sized massed attacks on Tan Son Nhut and Bien Hoa on 31 January 1968 changed the entire perspective of air base defense in Southeast Asia.[126/] They emphasized the insufficient numbers of security police, the lack of heavy weapons, and the inadequate training of USAF personnel in light infantry tactics throughout South Vietnam. The response to Tet was evident as 1968 progressed. Base defense priorities were raised, heavy weapons were procured, additional vehicles and night observation devices were obtained. Increases in security police forces were authorized, and special training in bunker and tower construction,

fencing, minefield emplacement, and infantry tactics and weapons employment were instituted.[127/]

Rocket patrols, rapid counterfire, free-fire zones, and sweep operations were all directed at decreasing the hazard of rocket and mortar
attacks. While these attacks continued in 1969, the number dropped
from 136 to 105.[128/] The number of rockets and mortars impacting on the
air bases also decreased from 983 to 439 and from 748 to 473, respectively (430 of the 473 mortar rounds in 1969 hit Phan Rang), indicating a
reasonable degree of success in these counter-rocket efforts.[129/] A program
was also instituted to provide organic intelligence collection and
analysis within a 10-mile radius of each USAF base in Vietnam.[130/]

Efforts to continue the post-Tet objectives in base defense remained throughout 1969. AFM 206-1, Local Base Defense Tactics and Techniques,
published on 30 June 1969, recognized the need for combat infantry
skills for security police.[131/] Nearly all areas identified in 1968 as
requiring improvement were corrected by 1969. Special emphasis was
placed on making air bases relatively safe from successful massive ground
attack and repelling sapper attacks. Security police were trained in
the use of new weapons and mortars, in small unit tactics, and in heavy
weapons. Efforts were continued to integrate the VNAF into base defense
on all levels.[132/]

The overhead aircraft shelter program (CONCRETE SKY) was instituted
in 1968 and continued through 1969. The program was successful in

reducing the number of aircraft destroyed or sustaining major damage. While 34 aircraft were destroyed in 1968 and 91 had major damage, the figures for 1969 were 6 and 10, respectively.[133/]

Development of shelters proceeded for several years on an experimental basis, and they had been used in Korea.[134/] The initial shelter purchase for the Southeast Asia program was the steel arch "Wonder" shelter which had proved successful in tests at Eglin AFB, Fla. Ten of these structures were contracted for and were on their way to Vietnam by 17 February 1968.[135/] (Fig. 28.) It was decided to cover these shelters with 12 inches of concrete which would make them sufficiently strong to withstand a 122-mm rocket impact,[136/] later changed to a 15-inch cover of 3,000 psi concrete.[137/] The program was subsequently expanded to 392 shelters.[138/]

Construction began on the first shelter in July 1968.[139/] The initial concept of construction was to have RED HORSE meet the entire requirement. It soon became evident that RED HORSE did not have sufficient capability and the construction firm of Raymond, Morrison, and Knutson (RMK) signed a contract to cover about 40 percent of the shelters.

Other changes took place during the construction process. The initial shelters were to be 68 feet long, 50 feet wide, and 28 feet high. The length was changed to 70 feet in May 1969 to accommodate a jet blast deflector.[140/]

Aircraft Shelters with Concrete Cover
FIGURE 28

Cost reduction was a critical item as the construction learning curve progressed. Initial estimates for completed shelters ranged from $50,000 to $75,000 per unit. These were refined over the learning curve to $18,517 by RED HORSE and $37,117 by the civilian contractor.[141] Thus the overall cost per shelter remained at approximately $27,000. Despite the cost, the value of the program was illustrated on 25 March 1969 when a 140-mm rocket scored a direct hit on an F-4 shelter at Da Nang. The fully armed F-4 inside was undamaged. This saving of a more than $2 million aircraft offset the cost of the 98 shelters at that installation.[142] The shelter program in Vietnam was scheduled for completion at the end of 1969. At that time, 382 of the proposed 392 shelters had been completed.[143]

Civic Action[144]

Seventh Air Force participated in Military Civic Actions (MCAs), an integral part of the GVN Pacification Campaign, which the Commander, 7AF, considered vital to the future of Vietnam.[145] MCAs were conducted to help the Vietnamese build a stable, responsible, and responsive system of community life as part of the MACV "One War" concept. The primary goal of MCA was a viable Vietnamese society which could defeat subversion and meet the social and economic needs of the people.[146]

As with a number of 1968 programs, Civic Action was greatly affected by the Tet offensive and its attendant destruction. Identifying with

GVN objectives, the ensuing recovery efforts were aimed at socio-economic improvement of conditions surrounding the people. Hamlet projects were oriented toward community goals. Air Force activity, aside from tactical airlift, was oriented toward material and technical aid, education, agriculture, and socio-economic assistance. An effort was also made to shift the emphasis to the Village Chief as the primary link in coordination with the government.[147/]

At the beginning of 1969, Civic Action was directed at community development with emphasis on operations in or near population and political centers, lines of communications, and economic installations. All operations were conducted with maximum Vietnamese participation, with special attention given to VNAF and GVN participation to help create a sense of identity between government agencies and other elements of Vietnamese society. Activities stressed were education, health, public works, refugee relief, village and hamlet administration, agriculture and animal husbandry, Chieu Hoi, youth, and housing.

Seventh Air Force MCA operations were centered around the main U.S. bases in Vietnam, generally within a 10-mile radius (the rocket belt). This made MCA a vital aspect of base security. Approximately 76 percent of the labor and 24 percent of the materials used in the projects were furnished by the people in the villages and hamlets, the highest percentage in all US/FWMAF MCA. Village and hamlet officials developed a much greater awareness of their role in community development. Altogether,

MCA operations with the Vietnamese directly or indirectly affected the economic, social, and political life of approximately 4,000,000 people in nine provinces.[148/]

Psychological Warfare Operations

During 1968, the psychological warfare operation was conducted by the 5th and 9th Special Operations Squadrons.[149/] Their resources included 25 O-2Bs, 14 C-47s, and 22 U-10s,[150/] and the average number of sorties flown was 2,481 per month.[151/] The role of the Air Force in the psywar effort was simply that of providing aircraft. Seventh Air Force fragged the missions, but the targets, along with leaflet and tape acquisition, were the responsibility of the Army.[152/] Also continued during the year until the bombing halt was Operation FRANTIC GOAT, a high altitude release of leaflets by C-130s to wind drift into North Vietnam. F-4 aircraft were also used in this effort.[153/] The overall psywar effort was reduced during the year by use of C-47s as flare aircraft during the night.[154/]

The basic psywar operation remained the same during 1969, except that the aircraft force was reduced when the 5th SOS was deactivated on 15 October.[155/] Prior to that date, approximately 14,500 speaker hours had been flown and about 2 billion leaflets dropped by averaging 1,734 monthly missions in 1969.[156/] The remaining force of 6 C-47s and 18 O-2Bs were located at Thuy Hoa, Bien Hoa, and Da Nang. These aircraft covered all of Vietnam and some of the Laos trail system. Two

77

FRANTIC GOAT missions per week were being flown at the end of 1969, with an occasional C-130 leaflet drop in South Vietnam.[157/] The VNAF continued to assume an increasing portion of the psywar effort with its U-17 and C-47 aircraft as the year progressed.[158/]

The results of the psywar effort were very difficult to determine. During 1968, there were approximately 18,000 Hoi Chanhs and during the first 9 months of 1969, about 33,000 Chieu Hoy returnees.[159/] It can be assumed that the psywar effort had some impact, since a number of defectors indicated knowledge of the leaflets which had been dropped.[160/]

Search and Rescue [161/]

The overall supervision, management, and control of Aerospace Search and Rescue forces assigned to Southeast Asia were responsibilities of the 3d Aerospace Rescue and Recovery Group (ARRG) at Tan Son Nhut AB. The group operated two rescue coordination centers, at Son Tra, Vietnam, and Udorn RTAFB, Thailand. (Fig. 29.)[162/] The organization's resources included 24 HH-3/53 long-range, air refuelable helicopters, 29 HH-43 local base rescue helicopters, and 11 HC-130P tanker/mission control aircraft.[163/] In addition, there were other resources dedicated to SAR, particularly the A-1Es from Da Nang (Spad) and NKP (Sandy). Many especially difficult SAR efforts required additional aircraft from throughout SEA.[164/]

The mission of the 3d ARRG was to aid persons in distress and recover survivors from hostile territory. The accomplishment of this

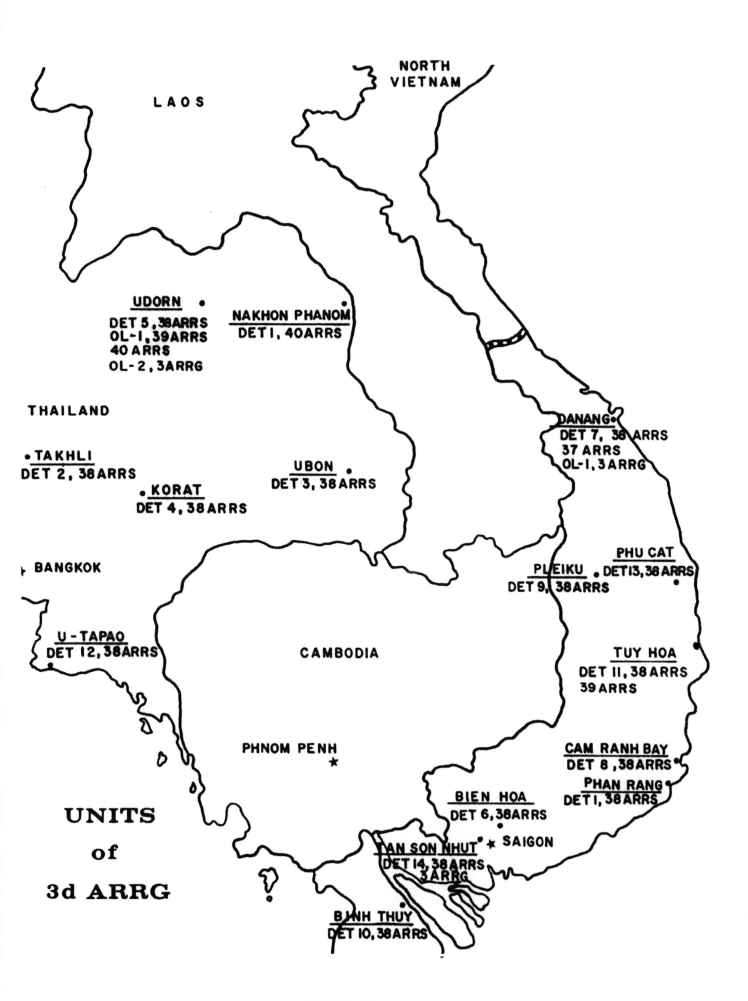

NORTH
VIETNAM

LAOS

UDORN •
DET 5, 38ARRS
OL-1, 39ARRS
40 ARRS
OL-2, 3 ARRG

NAKHON PHANOM •
DET 1, 40 ARRS

THAILAND

• TAKHLI
DET 2, 38ARRS

• KORAT
DET 4, 38ARRS

UBON •
DET 3, 38 ARRS

DANANG •
DET 7, 38 ARRS
37 ARRS
OL-1, 3 ARRG

⊦ BANGKOK

PHU CAT
PLEIKU • DET 13, 38 ARRS
DET 9, 38ARRS

U - TAPAO
DET 12, 38ARRS

CAMBODIA

TUY HOA
DET 11, 38 ARRS
39 ARRS

CAM RANH BAY
DET 8, 38ARRS •

PHNOM PENH
★

BIEN HOA
DET 6, 38ARRS

PHAN RANG
DET 1, 38ARRS

UNITS
of
3d ARRG

TAN SON NHUT •
DET 14, 38ARRS
3 ARRG

★ SAIGON

BINH THUY
DET 10, 38ARRS

FIGURE 29

mission required ground alert HH-43 and HH-3/53 helicopters and aircraft, as well as airborne, air refuelable HH-3/53 helicopters. In addition, HC-130Ps were maintained in orbit as a rescue coordination center and a refueling tanker for the airborne helicopters. Rescue Escort (RESCORT) Forces were required to suppress hostile fire in many rescues. This support was provided by the A-1Es, although use of faster and more survivable aircraft was being investigated in late 1969. On occasion, Rescue Combat Air Patrol (RESCAP) was also needed if there were a possible MIG threat during a SAR effort.[165/]

The strides made in Search and Rescue since the beginning of the Vietnam conflict have been outstanding. From a limited capability of HH-43 helicopters, HU-16s, and HC-54s, the effort has grown to the operation just described.[166/] The force's accomplishments have been impressive also. From 1 December 1964 through 30 September 1969, 2,747 successful rescues were made. While the majority of these saves were downed flyers, Army units, and seriously ill troops, even civilians have been rescued by the 3d ARRG.[167/]

The magnitude of some SAR efforts can be illustrated by one that took place in Laos on 5-7 December 1969. In that successful three-day effort to save one airman, a total of 332 sorties were flown, 21 different types of ordnance were used, and 10 helicopters and 5 A-1Es sustained battle damage. There were 1,463 bombs and antipersonnel weapons dispensed, not counting cannon and mini-gun fire.[168/]

Two areas of improvement in SAR forces were evident at the end of 1969. First, the need for a replacement helicopter for the HH-43. That light, short-range aircraft had served well in a base level SAR role but was unable to function in any sustained effort because of its short range and limited lifting power. Second, was the need to continue to perfect the night SAR capability. In many cases the AAA threat was lower at night but terrain and visibility made SAR attempts impossible. Consequently, it was standard procedure to discontinue a rescue attempt at last light until first light the following day. In late 1969, a Xenon floodlight, Low-Light-Level Television, and a Direct Viewing Device were being installed on the HH-53B helicopters at Udorn to provide some night SAR capability.[169/]

CHAPTER V

VIETNAMIZATION OF AIR WAR AND OUTLOOK

Introduction

After a meeting with President Nguyen Van Thieu on Midway Island in June 1969, President Richard M. Nixon announced that 25,000 American soldiers in RVN were to be redeployed by August. At the end of 1969, the President reiterated to the people of the United States, his determination to scale down American participation in the war. [1] The Paris peace talks had accomplished nothing substantive, while the enemy's ground actions in RVN had sputtered along at an unusually low level for 18 months. The administration did not commit itself to a fixed date for a total withdrawal of U.S. forces but proceeded with an incremental reduction of combat troops. [2] On several occasions, the President and the Secretary of Defense reaffirmed U.S. willingness to continue a combat advisory role to the GVN, but insisted that the combat burden itself must henceforth be borne in a larger measure by the Vietnamese. Vietnamization was the order of the day. The risks were apparent to everyone concerned, but the U.S. Government was clearly willing to assume the risks involved. The Commander, 7AF, placed renewed emphasis on the matter as 1969 ended: "Vietnamization, through enhancement of the RVNAF Improvement and Modernization (I&M) Program, is a task equal in priority and importance to the 7AF combat mission." [3]

Specific accomplishments to which the VNAF could point during the period included an intensive training program for helicopter pilots concurrent with the conversion of four of the five helicopter squadrons to the UH-1. This conversion greatly enhanced the capability of the VNAF to provide air mobility for ground combat troops. Of the three C-47 transport squadrons, one had been converted to C-119s in March 1968 and another had begun its modification to AC-47s in the summer of 1968.[4] In fighter planes as well, the modernization phase progressed, and three fighter squadrons were equipped with A-37s during 1968 and 1969.[5] VNAF involvement in the Tactical Air Control System was constantly and greatly increased, particularly during 1969. By the end of 1969, the conversion from USAF to VNAF in Aircraft Control and Warning (ACW) systems was well under way, with VNAF possessing an operational capability of 70 percent and full self-sufficiency predicted by the end of 1971.[6]

Significant advances were also evident in the amount and level of training. The size of the VNAF doubled during 1969, from approximately 17,500 at the start to about 35,500 at the end of the year.[7]

A major test of the VNAF came during the 1968 Tet offensive when more than half of the VNAF personnel were on leave at the moment the enemy struck. Ninety percent were back on duty within 72 hours and the force flew long and well in support of Allied operations. During the 17-day period of intensive fighting which began on 30 January, the VNAF flew more than 1,300 strike sorties.[8]

At the end of 1969, the major problems for the VNAF lay in the areas of training, the personnel reporting system, aircraft maintenance, and aircraft availability.[9/] The training problem was complicated by the great number of airmen involved, the precise technical knowledge required to operate sophisticated aircraft equipment, the need to send VNAF personnel to the U.S., and the lack of proper facilities. All problems were compounded by the English language requirement.[10/] But the thrust of the program was toward self-reliance, and the plans were directed to that goal.

Phase II Accelerated I&M Plan

As early as June 1969, a directive from the Secretary of Defense envisioned an expanded and self-sufficient ARVN and VNAF by 1974. The instrument for achieving this goal for the VNAF was known as "The VNAF Improvement and Modernization Plan," approved by Secretary Clark McAdams Clifford in December 1968.[11/] By early 1969, the timetable was moved up and the plan was revised into the Phase II Accelerated Plan. Operating under its guidance, the VNAF doubled in size during 1969, compressing the original time frame considerably.[12/]

Simultaneously, the modernization and upgrading of capability proceeded in all areas in spite of the problems encountered in train-ing--the most serious of the problem areas.[13/] During 1969, major USAF operations ended at Nha Trang in October.[14/] The target date for complete turnover at Binh Thuy was November 1970.[15/] At Pleiku, 7AF units were already being phased out with the expectation that by late 1970, the only remaining U.S. flying unit would be a small FAC detachment.[16/] By

83

the end of 1970, the plan envisioned that three of the six shared air bases would be returned entirely to the hands of the VNAF. There were similar plans to transfer full control of the four Corps Tactical Zone DASC systems to VNAF at various points during 1970--IV DASC by the end of December.[17/] Coinciding with these moves was the plan to place major reliance for air base defense on the VNAF.[18/]

Organizationally, the VNAF plan called for a change from a wing level to a division level structure during 1970. The initial move in this direction was a redesignation and expansion of the 74th VNAF Wing (Binh Thuy) into the 4th Air Division, scheduled for April 1970.[19/]

Phase III

In December 1969, Seventh Air Force completed a study on how to further augment the VNAF size and capability. Not yet approved as the new year began, this plan envisioned 49 squadrons (as opposed to the Phase II goal of 40) and a VNAF of 1,283 aircraft and 43,700 personnel (as opposed to 930 and 35,000).[20/]

The proposed VNAF force structure under Phase III, if approved, would have the following aircraft:[21/]

Tactical Air Support
    (a) FAC/VR (0-1, U-17)   218
    (b) Gunships (AC-47, AC-119G)   36

VNAF A-1 Skyraiders in Formation
FIGURE 30

F-5 Freedom Fighter
FIGURE 31

Interdiction/Close Air Support

    (F-5, A-1, A-37)   258

Reconnaissance

    (a) Photo   10

    (b) ARDF (U-6)   8

Tactical Mobility

    (a) Fixed-Wing (C-47, C-119, C-123, C-7)   128

    (b) Rotary Wing (UH-1, CH-47)   528

Psychological Operations (U-17, U-6)   38

Unconventional Warfare   31

Training and Administration   28
(VC-47, UH-1, U-17, T-41)
                                   1,283

The Commander, 7AF, predicted that the VNAF capability to support counterinsurgency operations would show a significant increase in the early 1970s.[22]

Risks of Vietnamization

All predictions on the success of the Vietnamization program depended on a number of unknown factors. Most significant of these, of course, was the unpredictable level of enemy operations during the early 1970s. While the Phase II Accelerated Plan was directly geared to an assumed substantial decrease in enemy strength,[23] the Phase III proposal acknowledged the principal risk:[24]

> *"The subsequent phase down route to reach MAAG strength will affect risk during and after U.S. phase down. At the end of Phase III, VNAF will*

> *have 52% of current combined USAF/VNAF fixed-*
> *wing capability. This capability would only*
> *be able to maintain current level of activity*
> *by increasing sortie rates 93%. Thus the*
> *conclusion must be that a higher level of risk*
> *in comparison with present security achieved*
> *by present forces against high enemy activity*
> *levels is inevitable in FY 73 and subsequent*
> *years."*

Other significant questions raised in the Phase III Plan included

progress in pacification programs, risks to the economy of RVN, and

decisions regarding levels of U.S. forces--all unknown factors for 7AF

planners. [25/] The document raised the additional question of management

and leadership in the VNAF: [26/]

> *"Perhaps the most crucial risk factor in the long*
> *term is the viability of institutions of manage-*
> *ment. This factor is not amenable to mathematical*
> *analysis because in RVN it is largely based on the*
> *personality of a leader rather than the institution.*
> *The capability of the RVNAF to assume prime respon-*
> *sibility for the war is as yet untested. So far,*
> *the U.S. structure has held the developing RVNAF*
> *together as it has expanded. As U.S. presence*
> *is reduced, the RVNAF structure and institutions*
> *will be increasingly challenged by assuming full*
> *responsibility for national security."*

Examining the risks, the planners recommended flexibility in the

application of the phase down. It was necessary to gear the rate of

phase down to continuing and realistic assessments of VNAF capabilities.

For the first part of the decade, the evaluation of the risks involved

in USAF withdrawals appeared acceptable through FY 71. [27/]

As 1969 ended, MACV and 7AF planners moved to implement the

President's policy of disengagement of U.S. combat forces. The VNAF was meeting each challenge with good performance. COMUSMACV viewed the toughest and longest training job with Vietnamization as the one faced by the VNAF, but he noted with satisfaction that it was moving forward on schedule.[28]

CHAPTER VI

SUMMARY

Three significant events shaped the course of the war in Vietnam during 1968 and 1969. The first was the 1968 Tet offensive in which the enemy drew heavily on its resources, only to be seriously hurt and weakened. The second event was the stepped up interdiction campaign against the North Vietnamese LOCs in NVN and Laos. The third event was the introduction late in 1968 of COMUSMACV's pacification campaign which sought with considerable success to eliminate the VC infrastructure from the main population centers. For air operations, each event meant the steady application of pressure on the enemy. The bombing halts in 1968 and the troop withdrawals in 1969 notwithstanding, the enemy was not able to repeat the scale of the 1968 Tet offensive, and subsequent offensives were progressively weaker. In the last half of 1969, a lull was apparent in enemy initiated activity.

The 1968 and 1969 period was a time of development in air tactics and techniques, and a time of innovation, as seen in the single management of air, weekly fragging, aircraft shelters, base defense, and the interdiction campaign. Significant pressure was applied with the creation of specified strike zones, defoliation, night and all-weather bombing, and with the creation of zones free of enemy rockets (rocket belts) around air bases. The increased use of sensors and the application of new weapons further denied surprise and sanctuary to the enemy. It was apparent that air attacks inflicted severe damage on an already

88

strained enemy, destroyed significant portions of his resources, and made the supply routes dangerous and expensive for him. Strike aircraft, along with reconnaissance, airlift, FACs, and air rescue, all played their part in the efficient and successful employment of USAF/VNAF air resources.

These factors, combined with the cumulative effects of several years of bombing, produced the lowered scale of action. The large enemy losses suffered in Tet 1968, the out-country interdiction campaigns, and the extension of GVN control throughout the countryside provided an increasingly favorable climate in which both U.S. and GVN forces could operate.

FOOTNOTES*

CHAPTER I

1. (S) Interview, Gen Creighton W. Abrams, COMUSMACV, by Kenneth Sams and Maj Philip D. Caine, 3 Mar 70. (Hereafter cited: Abrams Interview.)

2. (S) Interview, Gen George S. Brown, Comdr, 7AF, by Kenneth Sams and Lt Col Richard F. Kott, 30 Mar 70. (Hereafter cited: Brown Interview.)

3. Ibid.

4. (S) Msg, Gen George S. Brown, Comdr, 7AF, to all Comdrs, 101045Z Jan 69. (Hereafter cited: Brown Msg, 101045Z Jan 69.)

5. (S) Abrams Interview.

6. Ibid.

7. Ibid.

8. (S) Brown Msg, 101045Z Jan 69.

9. (S) Abrams Interview.

10. Ibid.

11. Ibid.

12. Ibid; Brown Interview.

13. Ibid.

14. (S) Brown Interview.

15. Ibid.

* All extracts from TOP SECRET documents have a classification no higher than SECRET.

CHAPTER II

1. (S/NF)   Periodical, CINCPAC, "Measurement of Progress in South-
            east Asia," 30 Jun 69, pg 1. (Hereafter cited: "Measure-
            ment of Progress.")

2. (S)   Extract from Input, Rprt, 7AF, DI, "Sect A, Introduction
            and Statement of Objectives," (Part of Proj CHECO Year-
            End Review Case File), 1968.

3. (S)   OPlan, 7AF, "Seventh Air Force OPlan 498-1969, Combined
            Campaign Plan 1969," Basic Plan, 1 Jan 69, pg 2-3.

4. (S)   Plan, Hq 7AF, DPLP, "FY 72 Force Improvement Plan," pg A-7.
            (Hereafter cited: "FY 72 FIP.")

5.   Ibid.

6. (S)   CHECO Rprt, Hq PACAF, DOTEC, "TACC Fragging Procedures,"
            15 Aug 69, pg 15.

7.   Ibid/

8. (S)   CHECO Rprt, Hq PACAF, DOTEC, "Command and Control 1966-
            68," 1 Sug 69, pp 15-17.

9.   Ibid, pp 31-32, 36;
   (S)   Interview, Lt Col E. F. Borsare, Senior Duty Officer,
            7AFCC (BLUE CHIP), 10 Feb 70.

10. (U)   Article, Aviation Week and Space Technology, "Over 4,000
            u.S. Aircraft in Southeast Asia," 20 Feb 67, pg 19.

11. (S)   OPREA, CINCPAC CCS, "Recap Summary, by Aircraft, Within
            Service, Within Country, Month of 1-31 Dec 69," pp 6-10.
            (Hereafter cited: OPREA, Dec 69.)

12. (U)   Rprt, "Review of the Vietnam Conflict and Its Impact on
            U.S. Military Commitments Abroad," Report of the Special
            Subcommittees on National Defense Posture, House Armed
            Services Committee, H. Res. 124, pg 50.

13. (S)   Interview, Maj F. M. Logan, Jr., WSMC Liaison Officer to
            7AF, by Lt Col Richard F. Kott, 4 Feb 70.

14. (S)   OPREA, Dec 69.

15.
(TS/NF)   Ibid;
          Rprt, Hq PACAF, "Summary of Air Operations in SEA," Jan 68,
          Jan 69, Dec 69, Basic Plan in Three Volumes.

16. (S)   Interview, Comdr R. A. Hall, USN, Navy Liaison to 7AF,
          Ops Officer, 3 Feb 60. (Hereafter cited: Hall Interview.)

17. (S)   Rprt, 7AF, CPT, Management Analysis, "Command Status,"
          Jan 68, Dec 69.

18. (S)   Command Status, Dec 69;
    (S)   OPREA, Dec 69.

19. (S)   Input, DI to DOAC, Project CHECO Year-End Review Case
          File for 1968, 21 Nov 68, Annex D, Special Ops, pg 51.

20. (S)   CHECO Rprt, Hq PACAF, DOTEC, "OV-10 Operations in SEA,"
          15 Sep 69, pg 1. (Hereafter cited: "OV-10 Operations
          in SEA.")

21. (S/NF) Rprt, TAC (WC), Nellis AFB, Nev., "Final Report, COMBAT
          LANCER," Vol I, pg B-11.

22.   Ibid, pg A-1.

23. (S)   Command Status, Jan 68, Dec 69, pp Personnel, F-Sections.

24.   Ibid.

25.   Ibid.

26. (S)   Mgmt Summary, USAF, "SEA," 9 Jan 60, pg SEA 2-4. (Here-
          after cited: USAF Management Summary, SEA.)

27.   Ibid, pg SEA 2-36.

28. (S)   Input to DOAC, MACV, "The Air Campaign in NVN and Laos,"
          1968.

29. (S)   Hall Interview.

30. (S)   FIP, FY 72, pg D-7.

31. (S)   Rprt, DOA, Hq 7AF, "COMMANDO HUNT," 20 May 69, pg vi;
    (TS/NF) Hist Rprt, MACV, "Command History, 1968," Vol I, pp 409-411.
          (Hereafter cited: Command History, MACV, 1968.)

32. (S)   CHECO Rprt, Hq PACAF, DOTEC, "Khe Sanh (Operation NIAGARA),"
          13 Sep 68.

33. (TS/NF)   Command History 1968, pp 384-388.

34.   Ibid, pp 388-401.

35. (S)   Memo, AFGP Ops Staff Advisor (TACS) to Dep Chief, AFGP,
             "VNAF TACS Progress Toward Self-Sufficiency," undated
             (Late 1969).
    (C)   End-of-Tour Rprt, Col J. C. Neill, USAF, DO, for AFGP-
             CCH, 3 Nov 69.

36. (S)   Command Status, Dec 68, Dec 69;
    (S/NF)   Measurement of Progress, 1968, 1969.

37. (S)   Interview, Maj C. F. Quimby, USAF, 1st Wea Gp, MAC, 7AF,
             by Lt Col Richard F. Kott, CHECO Writer, 6 Feb 70.

38. (S)   Rprt, Col B. K. Partin and 1st Lt D. T. King, DOA, 7AF,
             "Impact of In-Country Force Allocations on Interdiction
             Effectiveness," 6 Sep 68, pg 111.
    (S)   Interview, Gen Creighton W. Abrams, Jr., COMUSMACV, by
             Kenneth Sams and Maj Philip D. Caine, 7AF, DOAC, 3 Mar 70.

39. (S)   Command Status, Dec 68, Dec 69.

40. (S)   Computer Data, Subprogram I.D., IS, SEADAB 447, 1 Jul 68
             thru 31 Dec 69. (Day Attack Sorties; Night Attack Sorties.)

41. (S)   USAF Management Summary, pg SEA 2-38.

42. (S)   Command Status, pp B-5, B-6.

43. (S)   Interview, Capt W. E. McCarron, USAF, Tng Off Advisor,
             74th VNAF Wing, Binh Thuy AB, RVN, by Lt Col R. F. Kott,
             CHECO Writer, 6 Feb 70.

44. (S)   FIP FY 72, pg I.

45. (S)   Interview, Gen George S. Brown, 7AF Comdr, by Kenneth Sams
             and Lt Col Richard F. Kott, DOAC, 30 Mar 70.

CHAPTER III

1. (S)   Memo for Record, Gen. W. W. Momyer, 7AF Comdr, subj: Meeting with Gen W. C. Westmoreland, 5 Feb 68. (CHECO Microfilm S-196 FR 009)

2. (S)   Msg, COMUSMACV to Comdr, 7AF and Others, 220448Z Jan 68 (CHECO Microfilm S-196 FR 105).

3. (S)   CHECO Rprt, Hq PACAF, DOTEC, "Khe Sanh (Operation NIAGARA)," 12 Aug 68.

4. (S)   CHECO Rprt, Hq PACAF, DOTEC, "Air Response to the Tet Offensive", 12 Aug 68.

5. (U)   Hoopes Rprt.

6. (U)   Ibid.

7. (S)   Ltr, MACEVAL, subj: "An Analysis of the Khe Sanh Battle," 5 Apr 68.

8. (C)   Interpretation of Captured Enemy Document, CDEC, USMACV: Bulletin 11,456, Doc Log 04-2278-68, 29 Feb 68 (S-196).

9. (C)   Ibid;
   (C)   Bulletin 439, Doc Log 04-2244-68.

10. (S)   Abrams Interview.

11. (S)   Brown Interview.

12. (U)   Summary 1968, Office of Information, USMACV, 1 Mar 69.

13. (U)   Ibid.

14. (S/NF) Rprt, Hq PACAF, DOTE, "Southeast Asia Air Operations, May 1968," Jun 68.

15. (U)   Summary 1968, Office of Information, USMACV, 1 Mar 69.

16. (U)   Ibid.

17. (S)   Ltr, 7AF (TACD), subj: Request for Input, 18 Nov 68.

18. (S)   Draft Working Paper, subj: Interdiction, undated.

19. (S) CHECO Rprt, Hq PACAF, "USAF Support for Special Forces in SEA," 10 Mar 69.

20. (S) Ltr, 7AF (DIP), subj: Request for Input, 21 Nov 68.

21. (S) Draft, Working Paper, subj: Interdiction, undated.

22. (S/NF) Rprt, Brig Gen George J. Keegan, DCS Intel, Hq 7AF, "7AF Summer Interdiction Program 1968";
    (S) CHECO Rprt, Hq PACAF, DOTEC, "Interdiction in RP I, 1968," 30 Jun 69.

23. (S) Rprt, 7AF, DOA, "COMMANDO HUNT," 20 May 69, pg ii. (Hereafter cited: COMMANDO HUNT.)

24. Ibid.

25. Ibid.

26. Ibid, pg vi.

27. Ibid, pg vii.

28. (S) Rprt, ASI, Maxwell AFB, "The Air Interdiction Campaign, 1 Nov 68-31 May 69," Dec 69.

29. Ibid.

30. (S) COMMANDO HUNT.

31. (S) Abrams Interview.

32. (TS/NF) Command History, MACV, 1968, Vol I, pp 26-27.

33. Ibid, pg 32.

34. Ibid, pg 33.

35. Ibid;
    (S) Directive, RVN Prime Minister's Office, Central Pacification and Development Council, "Basic Directive on 1969 (1970) Pacification and Development Plan," (1969, 1970) pp 1-4.

36. (S/NF) Ltr, 7AF (DOT), subj: Input, 4 Jan 70.

37. (TS) Rprt, J3-053, USMACV, subj: Historical Summary for Aug 69, 13 Sep 69.

38. (TS) Msg, JCS to CINCPAC, subj: Project 703, 012159Z Oct 69.

39. (S) Msg, COMUSMACV to CG, I FFV, subj: Gunship/Flareship
         Availability, 210545Z Dec 69.

                          CHAPTER IV

1. (S)   "OV-10 Operations in SEA."

2.   Ibid, pg 1.

3.   Ibid, pp 7, 8.

4.   Ibid, pg 3.

5. (S)   Ibid, pg 12;
   (C)   Exercise Directive 1, TACC, MISTY BRONCO, Armed OV-10A
         Evaluation, Jul 69.

6. (C)   Exercise Directive 1, TACC, MISTY BRONCO, Armed OV-10A
         Evaluation, Jul 69, pg 15.

7. (U)   Interview, Major Ragland, TACWFP, by Maj Philip Caine, 9 Feb 70.

8. (S)   Interview, Maj David Folkman, DOA, 7AF, by Maj Philip Caine, 2 Feb
         70.

9. (U)   Article, Air Force and Space Digest, Sep 69, pg 198.

10. (S) Rprt, Staff Visit by Lt Col Johnson to 469th TFS, 388th TFW,
         Korat RTAB, Thailand, 15 Feb 69. (CHECO MICROFILM TS-42,
         Frame 066)

11. (U) Article, Air Force and Space Digest, Sep 69, pg 210.

12. (S) CHECO Rprt, Hq PACAF, DOTEC, "Tactical Air Operations in SEA,"
         30 Jun 69, pg 94.

13. (S) CHECO Rprt, Hq PACAF, DOTEC, "First Test and Combat use of AC-47"
         8 Dec 65;
    (S) CHECO Rprt, Hq 7AF, DOAC, "AC-47 Operations," 14 Jul 66;
    (S) CHECO Rprt, Hq PACAF, DOTEC, "Night Close Air Support,"
         15 Mar 67;
    (S) Manuscript, Hq 7AF, DOAC, "The Role of USAF Gunships in SEA,"
         10 Dec 69;
    (S) Rprt, Input, Hq 7AF, DOO, "Gunships: Posture at Beginning of
         1968" (Project CHECO Year-End Review, 1968).

14. (S)   Rprt, TACAWG, Eglin AFB, Fla, "Final Rprt Gunship II," TAC
          OPlan 6, Feb 68.

15. (S)   Rprt, CPTM/DCS Comptroller, 7AF, "Command Status," Sep-Oct
          69;
    (S)   Rprt, Directorate of Mgmt Analysis, OSAF, "USAF Management
          Summary," 9 Dec 69.

16. (S)   CHECO Rprt, Hq PACAF, DOTEC, "The Role of Gunships in SEA,"
          30 Aug 69, pg 9. (Hereafter cited: "Gunships in SEA.")

17.   Ibid, pp 14-21.

18. (S)   Plan, Hq 7AF (DPLP), "FY72 7AF Improvement Plan", undated,
          pp 13-19.

19.   Ibid.

20. (U)   Manual, PACAFM 55-___, TACM 55-___, (Proposed), "Operations:
          Aircrew Operational Procedures - AC-119 and AC-130, 1969,
          pp 4-19.

21. (S)   "FY 72 Force Improvement Plan," pg 13-10.

22. (S)   Rprt, TACAWG, "First Report, Gunship II", TAC OPlan 6;
    (S)   "Gunships in SEA," pp 28-39.

23. (S)   Rprt, Hq 7AF, DOA, "COMMANDO HUNT", 20 May 69, 69-169, pg xix.

24. (S)   Background Paper, DPLR, SURPRISE PACKAGE, 17 Jan 70.

25. (S)   DCS/Plans Memorandum, Col Willard A. Nichols to C., 18 Jan 70.

26. (S)   Msg, CSAF TORUCDJFA/AFSC, subj: SURPRISE PACKAGE, 201611Z
          Jan 70.

27. (S)   Gunship Fact Paper, DOA, 22 Jan 70.

28. (S)   "Gunships in SEA," p 2.

29. (S/   Rprt, MACV, "USMACV Year-End Review - 1968," 4 Dec 68, pp 23-24.
 LIMDIS)

30. (S)   Interview, Lt Col R. A. Davidson, USAF Comdr, 3505th 14th SOW,
          by Maj R. F. Kott, CHECO Writer, Nha Trang AB, 8 Aug 69.

31. (S)   "Gunships in SEA", pp 2-4.

32. (S)   Form 7, Hq 7AF to DMX, 1 Oct 68-31 Dec 68;
    (S)   Input, DOO, Air War, Vietnam, 1968, Annex M, "Combat Tests
            of New Weapons Systems;"
    (S)   CHECO Rprt, Hq PACAF, DOTEC, "Airmunitions in SEA," 15 Nov 69.

33. (S)   Ltr, DPLR to DOA, Requests for Inputs to CHECO Rprt, 10 Jan
            70.

34. (C)   Ltr, DOT to DOA, subj: Inputs to CHECO Rprt, 4 Jan 70.

35. (S)   Pamphlet, Hq 7AF, DOAC, Project CHECO SEA Digest, Mar 68.

36. (S)   Ltr, DPLR to DOA, subj: Request for Inputs to CHECO Rprt,
            10 Jan 70.

37. (S)   Special Study, Directorate of Air Munitions, 7AF, 1969 Muni-
            tions Proliferation Study, Mar 69.

38. (S)   CHECO Rprt, Hq PACAF, DOTEC, "USAF Support of Special Forces
            in SEA," 10 Mar 69. (Hereafter cited: "Support of Special
            Forces.")

39. (S)   Ibid, pp 11-12.

40. (S/   OPlan 443-69, 7AF, "Defense/Evacuation of U.S. Special Forces
    NF)   Camps," 4 Jul 68, pp 3-4. (Hereafter cited: OPlan 443-69.)

41. (S)   "Support of Special Forces;"
    (S)   CHECO Rprt, Hq PACAF, DOTEC, "FAC Ops in CAS Role in SVN,"
            31 Jan 69.

42. (S/NF) OPlan 443-68, pp 2-3.

43. (S/NF) Ibid, pg A-3;
    (S)   "Support of Special Forces," pp 57-58.

44. (S)   CHECO Rprt, Hq PACAF, DOTEC, "The Siege of Ben Het," 1 Oct 69;
    (S)   CHECO Rprt, Hq PACAF, DOTEC, "The Fourth Offensive," 1 Oct 69;
    (S)   CHECO Rprt, Hq PACAF, DOTEC, "Kham Duc," 8 Jul 68;
    (S)   CHECO Rprt, Hq PACAF, DOTEC, "Khe Sanh (Operation NIAGARA),"
            13 Sep 68;
    (S)   CHECO Rprt, Hq PACAF, DOTEC, "Battle for Dak To," 21 Jun 68.

45. (S)   "Support of Special Forces," pg 54.

46. (S/NF) OPlan 443-68, pg 2;
    (S)   "Support of Special Forces," pp 54-65.

47. (S/AFEO) CHECO Rprt, Hq PACAF, DOTEC, "Tactical Airlift Operations,"
             30 Jun 69. (Hereafter cited: "Tactical Airlift Operations.")

48. (U)   Telecom, Maj Philip Caine with Capt Ligen, 834th AD, 7 Jan
            70. (Hereafter cited: Ligen Telecom.)

49. (S/AFEO) "Tactical Airlift Operations," pg 51.

50. (U)   Ligen Telecom.

51.   Ibid.

52. (S/AFEO) "Tactical Airlift Operations," pp 27-28.

53. (S)   Rprt, 834th AD Management Analysis, "Tactical Airlift
            Performance Accomplishments, SEA," Dec 68, pp B-1, B-10,
            B-12, C-1, C-6, C-8, D, D-1, D-6, D-8, E-1, E-6, E-8;
            Ibid, Dec 69, pp A-2, C-2, C-4, D-2, D-4, E-2, E-4.

54. (S/AFEO) "Tactical Airlift Operations," pp 95-96.

55. (S)   CHECO Rprt, Hq PACAF, DOTEC, "Khe Sanh (Operation NIAGARA),"
            13 Sep 69, pp 73-74, 87.

56. (S)   Interview, Gen George S. Brown by Kenneth Sams and Lt Col
            R. F. Kott, 30 Mar 70. (Hereafter cited: Brown Inter-
            view.)

57.   Ibid.

58. (S)   CHECO Rprt, Hq PACAF, DOTEC, "Impact of Darkness and Weather
            on Air Operations in SEA," 10 Mar 69.

59. (S)   Interview, Major Foster, DOT, 7AF, 26 Jan 70. (Hereafter
            cited: Foster Interview.);
    (S)   Interview, Major Skeen, TACC, 7AF, by Maj Philip Caine,
            26 Jan 70. (Hereafter cited: Skeen Interview.)

60.   Ibid.

61. (S)   CHECO Rprt, Hq PACAF, DOTEC, "OV-10 Operations in SEA,"
            15 Sep 69, Figures 8-9;
    (S)   CHECO Rprt, "IV DASC, 1965-1969," 6 Nov 69, pp 23-26.

62. (S)   CHECO Rprt, "IV DASC, 1965-1969," 6 Nov 69, pp 26-27;
    (S)   Ltr, DOCOO, Hq PACAF to DOTE, subj: "The Air War in
            Vietnam, 1968-1969", (U), 5 Jun 70.

63. (S)   FIP, FY 72, pg B-8.

64. (S)   Interview, Maj Cliff Jackson (USMC), DOCFF, 7AF, by Maj
             Philip Caine, 27 Jan 70.

65. (C)   OpOrd 303-69, 1st MAW, III MAF, Da Nang AB, RVN, 1 Jan 69,
             Encl 2 to Tab D to APP I to Annex C;
    (S)   Msg, Hq 7AF to OUSAIRA/Vientiane, Laos, subj: A-6A Diane
             Weapons System, 070420Z Nov 69.

66. (S)   FIP, FY 72, pg B-11.

67. (S)   Skeen Interview.

68. (S)   Interview, Lt Colonel McClure, TACPAL, Hq 7AF, by Maj
             Philip Caine, 26 Jan 70.

69. (S)   FIP, FY 72, pp G-23 - G-26.

70. (S)   Ltr, DOE to DOA, subj: Inputs to CHECO Rprt, 11 Jan 70.

71 (S)   Form 4, 7AF, "7AF Combined Campaign Plan 1968, Quarterly
             Summary (FY 2/69), 11 Jan 69, Tab C, Annex 3, pg 3. (Here-
             after cited: Form 4, 11 Jan 69.)

72. (S/AFEO) CHECO Rprt, Hq PACAF, DOTEC, "The EC-47 in SEA," 20 Sep 68,
             pg 9.

73. (S)   Form 4, 11 Jan 69, Annex 3, pg 3.

74. (S/AFEO) CHECO Rprt, Hq PACAF, DOTEC, "The EC-47 in SEA," 20 Sep
             68, pg 12.

75. (S)   Form 4, 11 Jan 69, Annex 3, pg 3.

76. (S)   Ltr, DOE TO DOA, subj: Inputs to CHECO Rprt, 11 Jan 70.

77.   Ibid.

78. (S)   Ltr, DOT to DOA, subj: Inputs to CHECO Rprt, 4 Jan 70.

79. (TS)   MACV Command History, 1968, Vol I, pg 29.

80. (S)   Interview, Capt Rudolph Hansen, TACC, 7AF, by Maj Philip
             Caine, 28 Jan 70. (Hereafter cited: Hansen Interview.)

81. (S)   OPlan 427-69, 7AF, MSEAADR Air Defense Plan, 26 Jan 69,
             APP XI to Annex B, pg 4.

82. (S)   FIP, FY 72, pg I-20.

83. (S)   Hansen Interview.

84.   Ibid.

85. (S)   CHECO Rprt, Hq PACAF, DOTEC, "The Rescue at Ban Phanop,"
             8 Jan 70, pg 4.

86. (S/AFEO) CHECO Rprt, Hq PACAF, DOTEC, "Air War in DMZ, Sep 67-Jun
             69," 1 Aug 69.

87. (S)   Hansen Interview.

88.   Ibid.

89. (TS/NF) CHECO Rprt, 7AF, DOAC, "ARC LIGHT, B-52 Strikes, Jun-Dec
             65," 9 Oct 66;
    (TS/NF/ CHECO Rprt, Hq PACAF, DOTEC, "ARC LIGHT 1965-1966,"
     AFEO)   15 Sep 67;
    (TS/NF) CHECO Rprt, Hq PACAF, DOTEC, "ARC LIGHT, Jan-Jun 67,"
             22 Mar 68;
    (S)   CHECO Rprt, Hq PACAF, DOTEC, "ARC LIGHT, Jun 67-Dec 68,"
             15 Aug 69.

90. (S)   Input to Rprt, DI to DOAC, "Special Operations," Annex D,
             21 Nov 68, pg 41.

91. (S)   CHECO Rprt, Hq PACAF, DOTEC, "ARC LIGHT, Jun 67-Dec 68,"
             15 Aug 69, pp 5-9.

92. (S)   Rprt, 7AF, "Command Status Rprt, Sep-Oct," 1969, pg B-27.

93. (S)   FIP, FY 72, pg B-29.

94. (S)   Input, DI to DOAC, "Special Operations," Annex D, pg 51,
             21 Nov 68.

95. (S)   CHECO Rprt, Hq PACAF, DOTEC, "ARC LIGHT, Jun 67-Dec 68,"
             15 Aug 69, pg 30.

96. (S)   Rprt, Hq 7AF, DOAC to DO, subj: Special Report: In-
             Country Air Operations, 3d Qtr, CY 68, 9 Oct 68, pp 4-5.

97. (S)   CHECO Rprt, Hq PACAF, DOTEC, "ARC LIGHT, Jun 67-Dec 68,"
             15 Aug 69, pg 44.

98.   Ibid, pg 9.

99. (S)   Interview, Maj Mohr, MACV, J-2, by Maj Philip Caine,
               30 Jan 70. (Hereafter cited: Mohr Interview.)

100. (S)   Interview, Col Horace A. MacIntyre, USAF, Deputy Director
               Intelligence Production, by Lt Col M. J. Mendelsohn,
               4 Jan 70.

101. (S)   Msg, COMUSMACV to CINCPAC, "ARC LIGHT Sortie Rates,"
               15 Oct 68.

102. (TS)   CHECO Rprt, Hq PACAF, DOTEC, "IGLOO WHITE (Initial Phase),"
               31 Jul 68;
     (S/NF)   CHECO Rprt, (Unpublished), Hq PACAF, DOTEC, "IGLOO WHITE
               (Jul 68-Dec 69), 12 Jan 70;
     (S/AFEO) CHECO Rprt, Hq PACAF, DOTEC, "Air War in DMZ, Sep 67-Jun
               69," 1 Aug 69. (Hereafter cited: "Air War in the DMZ.")

103. (S/NF)   CHECO Rprt, (Unpublished), Hq PACAF, DOTEC, "IGLOO WHITE
               (Jul 68-Dec 69)," 12 Jan 70, pg 6.

104. (S/AFEO) "Air War in the DMZ," pp 25-29.

105. (S/NF)   CHECO Rprt, (Unpublished), Hq PACAF, DOTEC, "IGLOO WHITE
               (Jul 68-Dec 69), 12 Jan 70, pp 6-7.

106. (S/AFEO) "Air War in the DMZ," pp 35-38.

107. (S)   Rprt, 7AF, DCPG, "Systems Implementation Program," Apr 69,
               pg I-6.

108. (S/NF)   CHECO Rprt, "IGLOO WHITE, (Jul 68-Dec 69)," 12 Jan 70,
               pp 20-22, 42.

109. (S/NF)   Ibid, pp 40-44.

110. (S/NF)   Ltr, DOT to DOA, subj: Input to CHECO Rprt, 4 Jan 70.

111. (S/NF)   Ibid.

112. (S/AFEO) "Air War in the DMZ," pp 37-38;
     (S)   CHECO Rprt, Hq PACAF, DOTEC, "SEA Glossary," 1 Jan 70.

113. (S)   CHECO Rprt, Hq PACAF, DOTEC, "Herbicide Operations in
               Southeast Asia, Jul 61-Jun 67," 11 Oct 67.

114. (S)   Rprt, 7AF, "Combined Campaign Quarterly Report (FY 1/70),"
               Tab J, Herbicide. (Hereafter cited: Combined Campaign
               Qtrly Rprt.)

115. (S)   Ltr, TACD to DOA, subj: Request for Input, 4 Jan 69.

116. (S)   MACV Quarterly Evaluation, Jan 68-Jun 69.

117. (S/NF) Command Status, 7AF, Dec 68, pg B-21;
     (S/NF) Command Status, Sep-Oct 69, pg B-14.

118. (U)   Input, DOO, 1968 Year-End Review of Vietnam;
     (S)   Combined Campaign Quarterly Rprt.

119. (S)   Msg, 366th TacFtrWg, Da Nang AB, RVN to 7AF, subj: F-4D
             Defoliation Capability, 011130Z Feb 69. (CHECO MICROFILM
             210, frame 99.)

120. (S)   Interview, Lt Colonel Wilson, TACPSO, by Maj Philip
             Caine, 2 Feb 70.

121. (S)   Msg, COMUSMACV to 7AF, subj: Herbicide Project 2/2D/5/68,
             181635Z Jun 68. CHECO MICROFILM 210, frame 81.

122. (S)   FIR, FY 72, pg B-31.

123. (S)   Working Paper, Hq 7AF, Directorate of Tactical Analysis,"
             C-130 Burn Mission Operations," 30 Jun 68. (CHECO MICRO-
             FILM 114, FR 173.)

124. (S)   Msg, CINCPAC to RUEOJFA/JCS, 110225Z Sep 68. (CHECO
             MICROFILM 210, frame 88.)

125. (S)   Abrams Interview.

126. (S)   CHECO Rprt, "7AF Local Base Defense Operations," Jul 65-
             Dec 68, 1 Jul 69, pp 25-26. (Hereafter cited: Local
             Base Defense.)

127.   Ibid, pp 40-41.

128.   Ibid.

129. (U)   Log, Hq 7AF, Inspector General, Security Police Section,
             "Log of Enemy Attacks on U.S. Air Bases in Vietnam."
             (Hereafter cited: Log of Enemy Attacks.)

130. (S)   Local Base Defense, pp 8-52.

131. (S)   Local Base Defense, pg 6.

132. (S)   Ltr, IGS to DOA, subj: Requests for Inputs to CHECO
             Rprt, 31 Dec 69.

133. (U)   Log of Enemy Attacks.

134. (S)   Rprt, AF Weapons Lab, "Protective Construction for SEA,"
Dec 67. (CHECO MICROFILM S-68, frame 22 1/2);
    (S)   Working Paper, Nr 138, Office of Ops Analysis, Hq TAC,
Inexpensive, Quickly Erected Aircraft Shelters for Use
in Non-Nuclear War, Oct 67.

135. (U)   Memo for Colonel Dusenbury, subj: Contractors Delivery
Schedule (30 Shelters), 3 Feb 68.

136. (U)   Msg, I CINCILENGRGP to PACAF, untitled, 24 Oct 69.

137. (U)   Ltr, AFRCE-E from OICC/RVN, subj: Capping Aircraft
Shelters, 17 Dec 68.

138. (U)   Briefing Paper, "Project CONCRETE SKY," undated.

139. (S)   Briefing, Colonel Williams for Brig Gen Bennett, 7AF,
15 Nov 69.

140.   Ibid;
    (U)   Ltr, 554th Civil Engr Sq to CHECO, subj: Hardened Shelters,
6 Mar 69.

141. (U)   Paper, Hardened Shelters, 24 Feb 69.

142. (U)   Draft Work Sheet, "Shelter Costs," undated.

143. (C)   CHECO Rprt, Hq PACAF, DOTEC, "USAF CA in RVN," 1 Apr 68;
    (S)   CHECO Rprt, Hq PACAF, DOTEC, "Psychological Ops by USAF/
VNAF in SVN," 16 Sep 68.

144.   Brown Interview.

145. (S)   Ltr, DPLG to DOA, subj: Request for Inputs to CHECO
Rprt, 31 Jan 70.

146. (S)   Annex E, DPL, Input to 1968 Year-End Summary of Activities,
pp 59-62;
    (S)   Rprt, "7AF Combined Campaign Plan, 1968 Quarterly Summary
(FY 2/69), 11 Jan 69, Tab E, CA;
    (S)   Rprt, MACV, "Year-End Review, Vietnam, 1968," 4 Dec 68,
pg 47.

147. (S)   Ltr, DPLG to DOA, subj: Request for Inputs to CHECO
Report, 31 Jan 70.

148. (S)   Interview, Lt Col Wilson, TACPSO, 7AF, by Maj Philip
            Caine, 20 Jan 70. (Hereafter cited: Wilson Interview.)

149. (S)   Ltr, TACD to DOA, subj: Request for Input, 4 Jan 69,
            pg 3.

150. (S)   Command Status, 7AF, Sep-Oct 69, pg B-14.

151. (S)   Wilson Interview.

152. (S)   Ltr, TACD to DOA, subj: Request for Input, 4 Jan 69,
            pg 3.

153. (S)   Input, DOA, "1968 Air War Vietnam Summary," undated,
            pg 5.

154. (S)   Wilson Interview.

155. (S)   Form 4, "7AF Combined Campaign Plan, 1968 Quarterly
            Rprt (FY 3/69)," 12 Apr 69;
     (S)   Form 4, "7AF Combined Campaign Plan, 1968 Quarterly
            Rprt (FY 4/69)," 17 Jul 69;
     (S)   Form 4, "7AF Combined Campaign Plan, 1968 Quarterly
            Rprt (FY 1/70)," 17 Oct 69;
     (S)   Rprt, "7AF Command Status, Sep-Oct 69," pg B-14.

156. (S)   Wilson Interview.

157.   Ibid.

158. (S)   Form 4, "7AF Combined Campaign Plan, 1968 Qtrly Rprt
            (FY 3/69)," 12 Apr 69;
     (S)   Form 4, "7AF Combined Campaign Plan, 1968 Qtrly Rprt
            (FY 4/69)," 17 Jul 69;
     (S)   Form 4, "7AF Combined Campaign Plan, 1968 Qtrly Rprt
            (FY 1/70," 17 Oct 69;
     (S)   Ltr, TACD to DOA, subj: Request for Input, 4 Jan 69,
            pg 3.

159. (S)   Input, DOO, "1968 Air War Vietnam Summary," undated,
            pg 5.

160. (S)   CHECO Rprt, Hq PACAF, DOTEC, "USAF SAR, Nov 1967-Jun
            1969," 30 Jul 69;
     (S)   CHECO Rprt, Hq PACAF, DOTEC, "The Rescue at Ban Phanop,
            5-7 Dec 69," 8 Jan 70.

161. (S)   Ltr, DSR to 7AF (DOA), subj: 3d ARRG Input to CHECO
           Rprts, 6 Jan 70.

162. (S)   FIP, FY 72, pg H-5.

163. (S)   Ltr, DSR to 7AF (DOA), subj: 3d ARRG Input to CHECO
           Rprts, 6 Jan 70.

164. (S)   Form 4, 7AF, "7AF Combined Campaign Plan, 1968 Quarterly
           Summary (FY 2/69)," Tab H, Aerospace Rescue and Recovery.

165. (S)   CHECO Rprt, Hq PACAF, DOTEC, "USAF Search and Rescue,
           Nov 67-Jun 69," 30 Jul 69.

166. (S)   Form 4, "7AF Combined Campaign Quarterly Report FY
           1/70," 17 Oct 69.

167. (S)   CHECO Rprt, "The Rescue at Ban Phanop, 5-7 Dec 69,"
           8 Jan 70, pp 13-17.

168. (S)   FIP, FY 72, pp H-6-9.

169.   Ibid.

                        CHAPTER V

  1. (U)   Speech to the American Public, 3 Dec 69.

  2. (U)   Speech to the American Public, 15 Dec 69.

  3. (S)   FIP, FY 72.

  4. (S)   "MACV Year End Review for 1968."

  5. (C)   Ltr, AFGP to DOA, subj: Input for CHECO Report, 8 Jan 70.

  6.   Ibid.

  7.   Ibid.

  8. (S)   "MACV Year End Review for 1968."

  9. (S)   Ltr, MAC J3-053 to Deputy ACS, J3, subj: Areas of
           Improvement and Problem Areas in RVNAF, 7 Sep 69, pg 5.

10.   Ibid.

11. (S)   FIP, FY 72, pg K-4.

12.   Ibid, pg K-5.

13. (TS)   Plan, 7AF, "Vietnamization, Phase III" (Proposal Plan);
                  (Hereafter cited: "Vietnamization, Phase III.")
     (TS)   "Trends Indicators Analysis," May 69.

14. (S)   Ltr, DPL to DOA, subj: Inputs to CHECO Report, 7 Jan 70.

15.   Ibid.

16.   Ibid.

17. (S)   Ltr, TACD to DOA.

18. (S)   Ltr, IGS to DOA, subj: Request for Input to CHECO
                  Report, 31 Dec 69.

19. (C)   Ltr, AFGP to DOA.

20. (TS)   "Vietnamization, Phase III."

21.   Ibid.

22. (S)   FIP, FY 72.

23. (S)   TIA, May 69.

24. (TS)   "Vietnamization, Phase III."

25.   Ibid.

26.   Ibid.

27.   Ibid.

28. (S)   Interview, Gen Creighton W. Abrams, Jr., COMUSMACV,
                  by Kenneth Sams and Maj Philip D. Caine, 3 Mar 70.

APPENDIX I

INTERVIEW WITH GEN. CREIGHTON ABRAMS, JR.,
COMMANDER, USMACV

Airpower has played a critical part in our whole effort in SEA. The enemy has two logistics systems, one in Laos and one in Cambodia. The one in Laos is direct. Supplies are shipped from NVN. With Cambodia, materiel from China, Russia, and Eastern Europe goes to Sihanoukville for offloading and re-transit.

The air effort in Laos during the dry season was to interdict. In 1968, the program was successful. We know this, because when the dry season was over, he didn't have enough supplies in SVN to meet his purposes during the wet season. He, of course, planned for a certain amount of losses, but I think his losses exceeded what he had planned for his operations in upper II Corps and I Corps.

In 1968, the effort was also successful because of a good combination of pressure on the ground--finding the enemy's supply--and making him use it up, and the air interdiction in Laos. In Cambodia, we can't do anything until the materiel enters SVN.

Close Air Support

Basically, what we are doing is trying to run up enemy casualties with our firepower, and the biggest weight of firepower comes from tac air. And we also want to keep our losses down, again by tac air. This

108

also includes the B-52s which have been tremendous.

Of great importance for every phase of our operation is the integration of all-source intelligence for targeting, both pinpoint targeting and pattern targeting. Over this two-year period, all source targeting has been steadily and dramatically improved. Our goal is "steel on the target" and that takes good targeting. In the AF, this is especially important in the interdiction program.

Also, regarding CAS, you need an integrated all source intelligence on the ground and with it, you must have an integrated all-resource reaction to this intelligence, particularly with air, including tac air, gunships, and B-52s. These must be organized to strike so all of them can be applied and integrated. If so, it will be a terrifying and powerful blow over a short period of time. This, too, has improved significantly.

The air is really a powerful weapon. But to use this power effectively, you need both integrated all-source intelligence and an integrated all-resource reaction.

Fortunately, we've had centralized management of the air effort and this has been important to me personally. While air is powerful, it is also flexible. From this level, power can be moved with ease. For example, our arena includes BARREL ROLL, STEEL TIGER, and South Vietnam. Where the enemy puts the heat on, whether it's the Plain of Jars or

Duc Lap, it's only a matter of hours until tremendous shifts of power can be made. We realize it's not all that effortless on the part of the Air Force. You have to arrange for tankers and that sort of thing, but the whole system is geared to do precisely that, with no long warning to the enemy. It's done right away. The centralized control of the application of power is an important feature and a critical one for efficient use of power.

Airlift

You have the long-range airlift from MAC which is of importance in carrying high value cargo, passengers, medevac, etc. The airlift in-country, not only supplies, but of passengers and shifting of units, is also very important. For example, in late October 1968, on a Saturday evening at 1730 hours, we made the decision to move the 1st Air Cavalry from I Corps to northern III Corps. The move was to start on the following Monday and be done in 15 days. The first units moved were in contact on Monday afternoon in III Corps. This is amazing considering the proposal first came up on Saturday and the 1st Air Cav is a heavy outfit, with a lot of materiel, such as that required to support its 400 heli-copters.

The support of the CIDG camps could not be maintained without air-lift support. For example, Bu Prang and Dak Pek are almost entirely de-pendent on air. In those cases of emergency where airlanding is imprac-tical, we are able to airdrop and this is extremely important.

Reconnaissance

We have both photo and VR reconnaissance. We need the photo reconnaissance. In intelligence, every aspect has its part to play, each makes
its contribution to the total effort that can't be obtained somewhere
else. Photography is critical to targeting, not only regular photo,
but IR, color, camouflage, etc.

The FACs deserve a special word. In RVN and SL and BR, there are
FACs flying all types of aircraft to match the environment and these are
very important. For sensitive areas, such as the borders of Cambodia
and Laos, you're not in the ball game unless a FAC is there. He makes
sure you're doing what is authorized and not guessing. He takes the
guess work out of an operation. They've made a real professional contribution, because they are seasoned professionals. FACs don't get lost.

Defoliation

The defoliation role is declining in importance as we are beginning
to move into enemy areas and his logistical structure.

COMMANDO HUNT III

The enemy has been guided somewhat by his 1968 experience. He was
in better shape to start this year, despite the very bad weather of last
October. All of the North Vietnam logistical structure was in good shape.
He had moved his supplies to the border in readiness, had his fuel
storage areas ready, and had taken all necessary actions to get started
when the roads opened. In 1968, the bombing halt had just gone into

effect and he was not in this position. He didn't have a running start.

Also, he is bringing in SAMs and 100-mm guns to reduce effectiveness of air interdiction. There is also the problem of BARREL ROLL which drew off some of our assets. We believe that the effort in the Plain of Jars is designed to pressure the Laotian Government to stop our inter-diction of STEEL TIGER. We can't prove this, but we feel it, and have to act on it.

The enemy was getting more through this year than last year, especial-ly in January and February. The results of air action are higher this year than last year, because the enemy has more trucks in the system and we have more gunships which are great truck killers. Again, the 7AF targeting, based on all-source intelligence, is improved over last year.

Tet-Khe Sanh

Tet and Khe Sanh were a high point for the enemy, but not for us. The whole enemy structure--Main Force, Local Force, laborers, intelligence, guides, communications, supplies--all this was at a high point of effec-tiveness and made it possible for him to commit his forces. However, in terms of manpower, the enemy did not get hurt too badly. But he did lose quality, lose some of his experienced people. In 1968 and 1969, after Tet, we started getting into that whole enemy system with ground and air attacks, working for the attrition of the system. Such things as police activities, small unit actions, ambushes, etc., allowed for a concerted effort against the enemy's system. This caused the subsequent high points not to be met or to be reduced. Due to the effectiveness of our actions, the enemy logistical/management system was eroded.

Vietnamization

The VNAF has made each mark with good performance. The toughest and longest training job we have with Vietnamization is the one VNAF faces. It's a big job but it's on schedule. All the people in the system are moving along. There are some management problems. For example, you can't disregard the flying hour program. VNAF, with its advisors, have planned well, made a good analysis of the quality of its people. They have a basic plan to determine who will be the effective people. This will lessen the impact of the quality decline when it comes.

SOURCE: Gen. Creighton Abrams, Jr. interviewed by Kenneth Sams and Maj Philip Caine, Project CHECO, 7AF, 3 Mar 70.

INTERVIEW WITH GEN. GEORGE S. BROWN,
COMMANDER, 7AF

Q: What significant changes have taken place in the conduct of the air war in Southeast Asia since your arrival in mid-1968?

A: One primary change was a shift in the weight of effort; in mid-1968, we were flying 70% of our sorties in-country and 30% out-country. Now it's 55% out-country and 45% in-country. This change has only affected the strike sorties. Our allocation of airlift, recon, FAC aircraft has remained essentially unchanged.

The pace of the war in South Vietnam has slowed appreciably. In August 1968, there were four enemy divisions around Saigon--the 1st, 5th, 7th and 9th. General Abrams declared Saigon a "no-risk" area which meant that whatever was needed in this part of III Corps was provided and there were no questions asked. Since that time, the enemy divisions have been chewed up considerably and have been unable to work effectively. In the 1969 Tet offensive, the enemy couldn't get past Tay Ninh. They were pushed back and they suffered great casualties. Now they're up around An Loc and Song Be and back across the borders, although the 1st NVA Division has been moved to IV Corps.

As a result there was a marked difference in the allocation of the sorties provided to the out-country effort. From August to November 1968, we put the effort in Route Package I using everything that could survive there. We used the slow-mover in STEEL TIGER, plus those aircraft which were diverted from NVN.

In November 1968, when we began COMMANDO HUNT I, we put the effort on the trail although we were under great pressure from Ambassador to Laos, William H. Sullivan, who was calling for more sorties in BARREL ROLL, but he could present us with no real targets to justify the amount requested. They still don't talk in terms of targets there, only round numbers of sorties required. And we get no expression of how those sorties are used and what results they get. Here in South Vietnam, when the Army needs air, they describe the target. Up there, it's a matter of 100 a day or 200 a day. Until the fall of Muong Soui in June 1969, we kept sorties around 35 a day. Then we knew we needed a major effort and went up to 200.

There is a number beyond which you don't gain much with more air effort. That depends on the targets, and whether our strike aircraft can be controlled or not controlled. Most are controlled by FACs and they can handle only so many per hour--more sorties than that number would only be wasted. Just before the enemy hit in January and February 1970, we dropped the sorties to 80-90 a day. We're back again at about 200 around Long Tieng and I think we've turned the tide. Enemy forces have dwindled because of the constant pressure from air. I'm optimistic that we can hold the enemy until the rains come in six or seven weeks, and then he's going to have to fall back.

115

Another difference in our air effort concerns STEEL TIGER. Most people misunderstand what we're trying to do in STEEL TIGER. We know you can't completely stop the enemy with an interdiction program, but you can make it costly for him by bringing his total system under pressure, including his supplies, trucks, AA defenses, and his troops. Truck counts are not the only measure of how you're doing, nor are secondaries. It's the constant pressure that hurts him. We know he's got problems, though some people talk about 70%-80% trucks in commission rate. We can't even keep 80% of our own trucks going all the time with good roads and no enemy interruption. He's doing a fantastic job, though. Some of his materiel and people will get through no matter what we do. But you need that constant pressure from the air on his infiltration effort and a forced attrition of what he gets through by our ground forces, forcing him to fight or capturing his caches. For example, in I Corps last year, they were capturing something like 13 tons a day. Now it's being stockpiled on the border between Laos and SVN and being brought in by porters and bicycles. I've been talking with the CG, XXIV Corps, about getting out on the ground on this side of the border, especially around A Shau, and getting those caches of supplies that have gotten through. It's a two-ended task.

Q: What impact have air operations (both fixed-wing and rotary wing) had in the conduct of the war?

A: There is nothing done in this war which doesn't touch on the air effort in one way or another.

Q: How badly was the enemy hurt during Khe Sanh and the 1968 Tet offensive by air operations? Is his apparent decreased effectiveness today traceable to heavy losses during and since Tet?

A: Khe Sanh was the beginning of the end for the communists in their military operations in Vietnam. And there is no question that air was responsible for the enemy setback at Khe Sanh. During the Tet offensive, when the enemy got to Saigon and was not able to get the popular up-rising he hoped for and the government didn't collapse, the result was an emotional and psychological strengthening of the government as well as a weakening of the enemy. We are seeing the benefits of this today.

Q: To what degree do you consider air attacks a substitute for the major ground search and clear operations conducted in the past?

A: Tactical air and helicopter gunships are no absolute substitute for ground operations. The enemy today stays in his bunkers and he's hard to locate. Even ground units sometimes move so fast that they "go right over" him, that is, they miss him when he's underground. Getting at the enemy requires both an air and ground effort. The Army operations now are reconnaissance operations. If they make contact, they call on air. If it looks like the enemy is definitely there and dug in, they'll move in after the airstrike. The result has been reduction in U.S. casualties which is of great importance. We are often accused of wast-ing airpower, particularly on suspected enemy locations. A lot of these suspected enemy targets that we're called upon to hit flush the enemy out,

117

keep him off balance, and let the Army go after him aggressively.

Q: What was the impact of the March and November 1968 bombing halts
on the war in the Republic of Vietnam?

A: The March bombing halt was a serious mistake. There are only two
big pressures that are felt by the enemy--our strikes against NVN and
inflicting casualties on his forces in RVN. We removed one of these
pressures when we stopped bombing. It permitted the enemy to step up
the war in RVN and in Laos. All we got out of it were the Paris negotiations which are providing the enemy with a propaganda platform.
He's in Paris but there is nothing to negotiate. It was a serious mistake and it prolonged the war in RVN, in my opinion.

The November halt had a lesser effect but nevertheless, it did have
a direct effect on the war in the south. The terrain in Route Package I
was more favorable to an air interdiction program since many of the routes
were in the open and could not be bypassed as easily as in Laos. Now,
very simply, the enemy has a free ride to the NVN border.

Q: What is your assessment of the role of USAF reconnaissance in support of our objectives in SEA?

A: Photo reconnaissance is, of course, a key to our out-country work
and our targeting. It helps us assess enemy activities such as road and
pipeline construction, to find his truck parks and storage areas, and

118

to learn whether we hurt him or not. VR by our FACs is also a very prime consideration in both the in-country and out-country operations. The FACs are the eyes of our operations. They do a valuable job.

Q: What were the reasons, from your point of view, for the preemption of the enemy's August offensive in 1968?

A: The enemy's August 1968 offensive was preempted to a large extent by our interdiction program in Route Package I. He had to withdraw forces from I Corps due to interdiction in Laos and pressure on the ground in RVN.

Q: To what degree is the enemy increasing or decreasing his infiltration effort through Cambodia in relation to interdiction of the Ho Chi Minh Trail?

A: I haven't seen any change in infiltration in STEEL TIGER as a result of events in Cambodia. In recent weeks, the resupply through Cambodia has been shut off. He may have to revert to getting in supplies by sea, using trawlers and ocean-going junks. Back in 1967 or 1968, Gen. William C. Westmoreland told me there was considerable truck movement on Route 110 in the Tri-Border area, probably coming up through Cambodia. We do not see that now nor did we last year.

Q: How do you view the requirement for furnishing air support in BARREL ROLL as compared to interdiction in STEEL TIGER and air support in RVN?

119

A: Gen. Creighton W. Abrams, Jr., and I agree that requirements for air in the RVN must get first priority because we have U.S. troops fighting here. Second (and first at this time due to reduced enemy activity in RVN) is the STEEL TIGER effort which has a direct impact on the fighting in-country. Third is BARREL ROLL, but we can up the sorties there when required. Of course, operations in all areas tend to ebb and flow with the monsoons.

Q: Do you think the enemy increases pressures in Northern Laos to dilute the air effort in the Republic of Vietnam?

A: Ambassador to Laos, G. McMurtrie Godley, and General Abrams agree that the enemy effort in Northern Laos is directed toward forcing the GOL to have us suspend our air effort in STEEL TIGER. The five-point program presented by the Pathet Lao shows this. Its demand is an end to bombing of the Trail network, however, it was flatly rejected by the GOL.

Q: What is your assessment of the contribution of herbicide operations in RVN?

A: The only people who can determine effectiveness of the herbicide effort are the people on the ground who get the advantage of defoliation, who can see better and move easier. It's a difficult operation to assess when you consider fighter escort. Before we dropped the herbicide effort from 24 to 12 aircraft, it was taking a full fighter squadron a day to provide escort. It's an expensive operation and it won't win the war; it

120

does make life more difficult for the enemy. I would rather drop bombs than defoliants. It's the same with dropping leaflets. Tactically, the psywar program makes sense. You might get individual enemy soldiers to come over to the government. But to drop millions and millions of leaflets is overdoing it.

Q: How do you view the role of tactical airlift in operations in the Republic of Vietnam?

A: Tactical airlift is critical to everything that goes on in this war. Its value is indicated by the screams we get when we try to reduce it-- and we need to cut it back. We already have reduced it since I got here. In September 1968, we had 76 to 80 C-130s flying airlift in-country and now we're down to about 55. This has been due to more efficiency in using our airlift and the fact that there are less troops in-country. Airlift is absolutely essential to the support of the CIDG, to each of the four corps, to the movement of ammo, POL, and people.

Q: Are there any areas where air forces have not been able to handle assigned tasks in SEA?

A: We are still not as effective in putting ordnance on target in weather conditions as we should be. We have improved somewhat with LORAN on the F-4s which gives us a better capability than MSQ, but we have only one squadron. We plan to equip another one. The problem at night is not as serious as during bad weather, particularly because of our gunship capability. Our gunships are now experimenting with a beacon from which they can offset their firing. It is effective about 200 meters out. We need better flares and there is a SEAOR on it.

Q: What is your assessment of the Vietnamization program in terms of the Republic of Vietnam Armed Forces (RVNAF)?

A: There is no doubt that we will meet the training schedules, the activation of squadrons, and the equipping schedules of VNAF. With the VNAF and ARVN, there's a problem of leadership. When that is done, we'll have improved the Vietnamese Armed Forces, but their capability will be considerably less than what we have today. So our second task is to trim the internal security problem to a scale that the Vietnamese can handle. In the time we have left, however long that is, we must make pacification work. We must improve territorial security, strengthen the police, find and liquidate the communist infrastructure, and expand political, economic, and social development. We're making some progress. The communist recruiting has fallen extensively. As the Main Forces are being pushed back to the borders and into the jungle, the police and the territorial forces (the RF and PF) can come in to take firmer hold. We want to leave a security situation which the Vietnamese can handle. The CORDS people at MACV believe if elections were held today, the communists could get only four out of the 44 provinces in Vietnam. So time is not on their side. Getting those last provinces won't be easy. But in a secure situation, the VC don't pose any real political threat.

Q: To what extent, if any, has the air war in SEA affected fundamental AF Doctrine?

A: In regards to this war's influencing doctrine, we must be careful that we don't draw lessons from here that are out of context. We must realize that the enemy has no air capability outside of North Vietnam. This gives us some extra freedom to operate, letting us, for example, fly our tankers and ABCCCs with relative ease. This may not be the case in another war. If we had air opposition, the war would be far different in many ways. Actually, our existing doctrine has been strenghthened by this war.

Q: How has the Single Manager for Air concept worked out in SEA?

A: The Single Manager concept has been a great success and the man who realizes this most is General Abrams. It is essential when the chips are down, as at Khe Sanh. The Marines are still not fully "with it," but we don't make an issue of it. Specifically, they report that so many sorties are available, when in fact that is about half of what are actually flown. But I have no doubt that when the chips are down, they would participate fully.

Q: How do you assess the accomplishments of the in-country interdiction program?

A: There's been a drop in the in-country interdiction. Our in-country interdiction program on the border of I and II Corps forces the enemy to resort mainly to the use of porters and bicycles.

Q: What is the relative effectiveness of preplanned in-country strikes versus immediates?

A: With the low level of enemy activity today, we aren't doing more with our preplans than keeping the system oiled. The immediates are more important than preplans because they are generally real time situations. Sometimes the Army will call for immediates when they can't get the preplans, so they can carry out some special operation like preparing an LZ. We are under heavy pressure from Washington to cut sorties and ammunition, but this must be done with caution. We would take more casualties if our troops had to go after all suspected enemy locations they now call air in to hit.

Q: What are your views on the command and control set-up in BARREL ROLL?

A: Command and control in the BR is weak. The Ravens are our best FACs, but they don't give a damn about paperwork and reporting and we don't know what's happening with our strikes. Sometimes they're using them on targets remote from the main action where they are needed. The nuts and bolts of command and control are the same in BARREL ROLL as in the rest of the theater. But it's not as tight there. In STEEL TIGER, we know what's there and what is being done, and operations are coordinated and carefully watched. That's not the case in BARREL ROLL.

Q: Has it been possible to provide Gen. Vang Pao with the sorties he believed he needed?

A: We think we're providing enough sorties but Vang Pao doesn't always think so. When I talked with Vang Pao last October, he said, "Americans like KBA. Buddhists no like. American pilots like KBA and we like American pilots." It's a great comfort for them to have radio contact with a pilot overhead and they think the way to get more air is by inflating KBA. We had nothing like the fantastic KBA that was reported last fall. The figures were badly inflated. Sometimes they ask us for 200 sorties a day. We ask them to give us firm targets which they can't always do. And they can't control all the sorties they get. The Ravens can handle only so many. Our most effective sorties are in STEEL TIGER. But right now, we're getting some good results at Long Tieng in support of Vang Pao's troops there. I'm optimistic and I think we'll be able to turn the tide there. The enemy troops are out at the end of a long logistics system. And we're hitting it at both ends.

In-country, our strikes are marginally effective between major battles and campaigns, for example, between a Ben Het and a Dak To. But when these major battles come, air is critically effective.

Our big problem in BR when Vang Pao was driven from the PDJ was weather. We could only work about six hours a day and usually there was haze that reduced visibility. Also, Vang Pao's troops didn't put up enough resistance when the enemy launched his attack this year, so as to force him to concentrate and create usable targets for airstrikes.

There has been good rapport between Ambassador Godley and Maj. Gen. Robert L. Petit, Deputy Commander, 7AF/13AF, and the Ambassador relied heavily on General Petit in matters of air support in BARREL ROLL.

SOURCE: Gen. G. S. Brown interviewed by Kenneth Sams and Lt Col Richard Kott, 30 Mar 70 (Rev. 2 Apr 70).

APPENDIX III

CHRONOLOGY
1968--1969

1968

January

15   Start of Operation NIAGARA, the air effort to defend the Khe
      Sanh Combat Base in I Corps.

23   President Lyndon B. Johnson ordered call-up of 14,000 Air Force
      and 600 Navy Air Reservists in response to the Pueblo crisis.

29   Start of Tet Offensive, later called the First Offensive.
      Between 29 January and 29 February, USAF support for free world
      ground operations ranged through the entire airpower spectrum from
      B-52 strikes to emergency airlift. Air followed the fighting
      from the countryside into and around the population centers
      throughout RVN, while keeping watch on enemy LOCs and base areas.

February

1   B-52 sorties increased from 800 to 1,200 monthly.

15   B-52 sorties increased from 1,200 to 1,800 monthly.

27   Gunship II (AC-130) flew first combat mission in SEA against
      trucks on the Ho Chi Minh Trail.

29   For the first time an ARC LIGHT strike was flown where the
      clearance limit was reduced from three kilometers to one.

March

4   Single Management for Air was instituted in RVN. MACV assigned
        7AF the responsibility of managing all USMC air operations,
        except helicopter and airlift activities.

15   Six F-111 aircraft moved from CONUS to Thailand to begin opera-
        tional tests.

18   7AF began fragging USMC aircraft under the Single Manager for
        Air concept.

20   Commando Super Sabre FACs (F-100Fs) stopped an estimated 150-
        200 vehicle truck convoy in an incident that became known as the
        Great Truck Massacre.

25   First F-111 sorties flown over NVN. Two aircraft were lost during
        the last week in March.

31   President Johnson ordered halt in the bombing of NVN above the
        20th parallel.

31   End of Operation NIAGARA. During the 70-day operation, U.S.
        airpower delivered nearly 96,000 tons of ordnance. Operation
        PEGASUS was begun for relief of the combat base.

April

1   Presidential order on bomb halt became effective.

19   Operation TURNPIKE, designed to impede the enemy's increased
        movement in Laos following the bombing halt, was begun.

May

5   Start of another major enemy offensive against Saigon, the May or Second Offensive, which spread throughout the country.

7   Start of Paris peace talks.

11   Death toll for week ending 11 May was 562, the highest of the war.

25   The first OV-10 Broncos bedded down at Bien Hoa Air Base.

June

28   Start of pull out from Khe Sanh.

30   The number of USAF personnel authorized in RVN was 61,132.

July

1   Start of Operation THOR in the southeast sector of the DMZ, aimed at reducing the threat from AAA and Artillery positions in the area.

12   Start of a one-month evaluation of COMMANDO SABRE control over night interdiction efforts.

14   Start of an interdiction program in Route Package I which continued until October.

31   OV-10 Broncos were deployed in SEA.

August

1   Gen. George S. Brown assumed duties as Commander, 7AF, and as Deputy Commander for Air Operations, MACV.

12   The OV-10 Bronco FAC aircraft directed its first strike in RVN.

18   Start of the enemy's August or Third Offensive, with attack-by-fire in III Corps, spreading with ABFs and ground assaults throughout RVN. This offensive showed the lessening combat capability of the VC/NVA, which had taken heavy losses during TET and again in May.

31   Tan Son Nhut became the busiest airport in the world with a total of 77,901 aircraft movements during the month.

September

6   F-111 deployment in SEA extended from September to 31 October.

6   Start of Stormy FAC missions, using F-4s, which gathered intelligence data and directed airstrikes against targets in NVN and Laos.

13   First hostile death in Thailand.

21   TROPIC MOON I evaluation completed.

29   Start of BLACK SPOT evaluation, a project involving an NC-123 aircraft equipped with sensor/attack systems to combat enemy vehicles along LOCs in Laos.

30   USAF strength in RVN was 61,405.

October

4   First KC-135 lost in SEA.

20-30 End of Project COMBAT TRAP, a test which involved 10,000-lb. bombs dropped from C-130 aircraft to create instant helicopter landing zones.

31   Project COMBAT BRONCO completed. Following the evaluation, OV-10s were assigned to operational units.

November

1   All air, naval, and artillery bombardment of NVN was stopped by order of President Johnson. Reconnaissance continued and increased emphasis was placed upon the enemy's LOCs.

11   The USAF took part in Operation LIBERTY CANYON, the movement of the entire U.S. 1st Cavalry Division from I Corps to an area north of Saigon.

15   Operation COMMANDO HUNT implemented to interdict enemy supply lines through Laos into RVN. Task Force Alpha was delegated the responsibility of bombing lucrative truck parks.

15   U.S. Navy aircraft, formerly bombing in NVN, started strikes in Laos, and ARC LIGHT strikes increased there. Between 15 November and 31 December, 838 B-52 sorties were flown in support of COMMANDO HUNT and in STEEL TIGER South (below 16' 30' N latitude).

17   First F-4E aircraft arrived in SEA.

November

22   Five F-111 aircraft departed SEA for CONUS.

December

4   CINCPACAF announced a policy that Wing Commanders assigned to SEA must have prior Wing Commander or Vice Commander experience.

11   All 7AF Wing and Base Commanders were alerted to increased enemy offensive and the possibility of attacks-by-fire. By 14 December, U.S. preemptive actions kept the enemy from gaining a favorable attack posture.

12   B-52s pounded the enemy LOCs and base areas threatening Saigon.

19   Combat sorties in SEA exceeded one million in 1968.

22-27   First AC-119G gunships arrived and deployed in RVN.

24-25   Christmas truce.

28   ARRS combat saves in SEA surpassed 1,500.

31   AC-119 gunship flew first mission in RVN.

31   B-52 sortie rate was 1,800 per month.

31   USAF authorized strength in RVN was 61,579.

1969

January

2   AC-119G gunship began combat air patrols in RVN.

10   End of BLACK SPOT evaluation.

22   Start of a new interdiction concept using 16 F-4 aircraft strik-
     ing selected road segments with road-cutting ordnance.

22   USAF directed the establishment of a Deployable Automatic Relay
     Terminal (DART) in SEA. It was designed to monitor sensor fields
     through an airborne or ground data relay platform.

23   Total USAF aircraft losses in SEA exceeded 1,500.

25   Start of Operation SEARCH, designed to exploit the combined
     talents of FAC, reconnaissance, and strike resources by flying
     both low- and high-level reconnaissance missions off the main
     enemy LOCs and into smaller roads and trails.

February

1   End of 60-day evaluation of F-4E aircraft.

13   Start of KEEPOUT operations in western III Corps, using special
     ordnance dropped on the main enemy LOCs along the Cambodian
     Border and extending toward Saigon.

15   Daily bombing of all interdiction points slowly phased out.
     Instead, packages of mine-type munitions were placed at key choke

points on LOCs which were supporting heavy traffic.

February

19-22   BOWIE WINNER operations were carried out in War Zone D, northeast of Bien Hoa, against an enemy staging and assembly area.

23   Start of a new enemy offensive, the Fourth Offensive, with wide-spread attacks-by-fire and limited ground probes.

26   The major enemy ground assault of the Fourth Offensive took place at Bien Hoa, a few kilometers from the air base, while ABFs and limited ground probes continued throught RVN. The enemy was unwilling or unable to mount actions on the scale of the three previous offensives but carried out a series of high-points until early April.

March

1   Project DART began operation at Bien Hoa AB.

3-4   USAF aircraft destroyed Soviet-built PT-76 tanks attacking the Ben Het CIDG camp in western II Corps.

16   New day VR sectors and night VR routes were implemented: the day reconnaissance program concentrated on wide areas and the night program on LOCs.

21   Project GRAND SLAM was initiated to provide comprehensive KA-1 area coverage of the DMZ and north to 17' 10" to search for enemy activity.

March

29 American deaths in SEA exceeded the Korean toll--33,642 as compared with 33,629.

April

27 A fire at the USMC Ammunition Supply Point at Da Nang AB spread rapidly, resulting in high-order explosions and fires. The loss in USAF, USMC, and VNAF munitions was calculated at $25.5 million.

30 The enemy to friendly KIA ratio increased to 9.2 to 1, the highest of the war.

May

11-14 VC/NVA initiated another high point in activity with 63 ABFs and 64 ground probes.

12 AC-123 aircraft operations were discontinued and the aircraft returned to CONUS for modification.

1-30 A VC/NVA operation was begun to isolate and overrun the Bet Het SF/CIDG camp near the Tri-Border area in western II Corps. The USAF countered with airpower ranging from B-52 strikes to gunship support.

1-30 A major B-52 campaign carried out against an enemy base area west of the A Shau Valley in I Corps.

June

7   President Richard M. Nixon met with President Thieu at Midway to discuss war in RVN. Withdrawal of 25,000 U.S. troops was ordered from RVN by September.

13   The last of seven Air National Guard units deployed to RVN was returned to CONUS.

1-30 VC/NVA continued attempt to take Ben Het. USAF defense effort countered the threat, striking enemy troops and LOCs throughout the Tri-Border area and in the immediate vicinity of the camp.

July

3   VC/NVA withdrew from the Ben Het area, unable to achieve their goal of overrunning the camp.

8   Start of Operation KEYSTONE EAGLE, the withdrawal of 25,000 U.S. troops from SEA.

22   ARC LIGHT sorties were reduced from 1,800 to 1,600 per month.

August

29   Operation KEYSTONE EAGLE redeployment was completed.

September

2   Death of Ho Chi Minh.

8   Three-day cease-fire in honor of Ho Chi Minh.

136

September

16   Announcement was made of Operation KEYSTONE CARDINAL, the withdrawal of 35,000 additional U.S. troops from SEA by 15 December.

21   Start of KEYSTONE CARDINAL.

30   President Nixon announced decision to redeploy 6,000 military personnel from Thailand by 1 July 1970.

October

1   Four VNAF H-34 squadrons converted to UH-1s became operationally ready. First VNAF helicopter (UH-1) class was graduated from the Defense Language Institute English Language course at Lackland AFB.

6   VNAF C-47 gunship squadron provided from USAF resources became operationally ready.

15-20   Start of VC/NVA operations in the Bu Prang/Duc Lap area in southern II Corps, which attempted to isolate and overrun one of the camps. The enemy units were identified as those which had besieged Ben Het.

20   The last standard configuration AC-130 gunship was deployed to Ubon AB, Thailand, to provide additional self-contained night attack systems.

29   The Office of Special Assistant for Vietnamization was established to serve as the Air Staff focal point for Vietnamization matters.

137

November

15   Headquarters USAF approved deployment of SURPRISE PACKAGE AC-130A Gunship II aircraft to arrive in SEA by early December for combat evaluation.

24   All F-105 aircraft in SEA (four tactical fighter squadrons) were consolidated at Takhli AB, Thailand, to increase management efficiency.

December

8-22   Enemy offensive activity around Bu Prang/Duc Lap lessened, although minor contacts continued and free world installations in the area received ABFs.

15   President Nixon announced withdrawal of 50,000 additional troops from SEA by 15 April 1970.

25   Christmas cease-fire.

24-31   Total U.S. military personnel deaths attributed to hostile action in SEA exceeded 40,000.

NOTE: CHECO Rprt, Hq PACAF, DOTEC, "SEA Glossary 1961-1970," 1 Jan 70, provides reference data pertinent to operations and projects.

GLOSSARY

AAA	Antiaircraft Artillery
ABCCC	Airborne Battlefield Command and Control Center
ABF	Attack By Fire
ACW	Aircraft Control and Warning
AFCC	Air Force Component Commander
AGL	Above Ground Level
ALCC	Airlift Control Center
ALO	Air Liaison Officer
AOB	Air Order of Battle
APC	Accelerated Pacification Campaign
ARDF	Airborne Radio Direction Finding
ARRG	Aerospace Rescue and Recovery Group
ARVN	Army of Republic of Vietnam
ASRT	Air Support Radar Team
BDA	Bomb Damage Assessment
BR	BARREL ROLL
CAS	Close Air Support
CIDG	Civilian Irregular Defense Group
COMUSMACV	Commander, U.S. Military Assistance Command, Vietnam
CONUS	Continental United States
CORDS	Civil Operations and Revolutionary Development Support
CRC	Control and Reporting Center
CTZ	Corps Tactical Zone
DART	Deployable Automatic Relay Terminal
DASC	Direct Air Support Center
DMZ	Demilitarized Zone
DOD	Department of Defense
ECM	Electronic Countermeasures
FAC	Forward Air Controller
FACP	Forward Air Control Post
FIP	Force Improvement Plan
FSCC	Fire Support Coordination Center
FWMAF	Free World Military Assistance Forces
GMTI	Ground Moving Target Indicator
GVN	Government of Vietnam
IFR	Instrument Flight Rules
I&M	Improvement and Modernization
IP	Initial Point
IR	Infrared
ISC	Infiltration Surveillance Center

KIA	Killed in Action
km	kilometer
LAPES	Low Altitude Parachute Extraction System
LLLTV	Low-Light-Level Television
LOC	Line of Communications
LORAN	Long-Range Navigation
MAC	Military Airlift Command
MACV	Military Assistance Command, Vietnam
MAW	Marine Air Wing
MCA	Military Civic Action
MTI	Moving Target Indicator
NKP	Nakhon Phanom
NOD	Night Observation Device
NS	North Sector
NVA	North Vietnamese Army
NVAF	North Vietnamese Air Force
NVN	North Vietnam(ese)
NW	Northwest
PL/NVN	Pathet Lao/North Vietnam
PDJ	Plain of Jars
POL	Petroleum, Oil, and Lubricants
PSI	Pounds Per Square Inch
PW	Prisoner of War
RLG	Royal Laotian Government
RMK	Raymond, Morrison, and Knutsen
RP	Route Package
RVN	Republic of Vietnam
RVNAF	Republic of Vietnam Armed Forces
SALOA	Special ARC LIGHT Operating Area
SAC	Strategic Air Command
SAM	Surface-to-Air Missile
SAR	Search and Rescue
SEA	Southeast Asia
SEAOR	Southeast Asia Operational Requirements
SF	Special Forces
SL	STEEL TIGER
SLAM	Search-Locate-Annihilate-Monitor
SLAR	Side-Looking Airborne Radar
SMS	Single Management System
SSZ	Specified Strike Zone
SSW	South, Southwest
STOL	Short Takeoff and Landing

TACC	Tactical Air Control Center
TACP	Tactical Air Control Party
TACS	Tactical Air Control System
TASE	Tactical Air Support Element
TASS	Tactical Air Support Squadron
TCA	Traffic Control Area
TCP	Traffic Control Point
TDY	Temporary Duty
TEWS	Tactical Electronic Warfare Squadron
TFA	Task Force Alpha
TMA	Traffic Management Agency
TOC	Tactical Operations Center
TOT	Time Over Target
TSV	Tactical Secure Voice
UE	Unit Equipment
USMC	United States Marine Corps
USN	United States Navy
VC	Viet Cong
VCI	Viet Cong Infrastructure
VNAF	Vietnamese Air Force
VR	Visual Reconnaissance

Lightning Source UK Ltd.
Milton Keynes UK
UKOW020753230512

193107UK00004B/18/P